WHO AM I?

THE CHRISTIAN IDENTITY

I AM, WHAT GOD SAYS, I AM
I HAVE, WHAT GOD SAYS, I HAVE
I CAN, WHAT GOD SAYS, I CAN
I SHOULD, WHAT GOD SAYS, I SHOULD,
DO, IN JESUS CHRIST MY LORD.

REV. PABLO AROCHA

Copyright © 2024 Rev. Pablo Arocha.

All rights reserved. No part of this book may be reproduced, stored, or transmitted by any means—whether auditory, graphic, mechanical, or electronic—without written permission of both publisher and author, except in the case of brief excerpts used in critical articles and reviews. Unauthorized reproduction of any part of this work is illegal and is punishable by law.

All Scripture quotations, unless otherwise noted, taken from THE HOLY BIBLE, NEW INTERNATIONAL VERSION®, NIV® Copyright © 1973, 1978, 1984, 2011 by Biblica, Inc.® Used by permission. All rights reserved worldwide.

Scripture quotations marked (KJV) taken from *The Holy Bible, King James Version*. Cambridge Edition: 1769.

ISBN: 979-8-89031-979-1 (sc)
ISBN: 979-8-89031-980-7 (hc)
ISBN: 979-8-89031-981-4 (e)

Because of the dynamic nature of the Internet, any web addresses or links contained in this book may have changed since publication and may no longer be valid. The views expressed in this work are solely those of the author and do not necessarily reflect the views of the publisher, and the publisher hereby disclaims any responsibility for them.

One Galleria Blvd., Suite 1900, Metairie, LA 70001
(504) 702-6708

CONTENTS

Acknowledgment 1
Dedication 3
God's Holy Word 7
God the Father 11
God's 7 Covenant 25
God's Old Testament 27
God's 7 Dispensations 28
God's New Testament: A Dispensation of Grace 30
God the Son 33
God the Holly Spirit 38
Is the Baptism of the Holy Spirit for Me Today? 48
God's Plan for Man 51
Who Am I, My Identity, Writes and Privileges,
    And God Given Power. 69
God says, that I am (A new creature in Christ Jesus) 71
God says, that I am (Born of an incorruptible seed) 72
God says, that I am (Born again spiritually) 73
God says, that I am (A spiritual babe in Christ) 75
God says, that I am (A child of God) 76
God says, that I am (An overcomer in Christ) 78
God says, that I am (Delivered from the kingdom of darkness) ... 81
God says, that I am (The righteousness of God in Christ) 83
God says, that I am, (A member of Christ's body) 90
God says, that I am, (A Temple of the Holy Spirit) 94
God says, that I am, (An ambassador for Christ) 97

I Am a Chosen Generation, a Royal Priesthood, a Holy
    Nation, a Peculiar People, and to Show Forth the
    Praises of Him 101
God says, I have a full armor, (Faith), (believe), (Convictions) ... 114
God says, that I have, (A new life) 118
God says, that I have, (A divined nature) 119
God says, that I have, (A citizenship in heaven) 120
God says, that I have, (Bean made free) 122
God says, that I have, (His leadership for triumph) 123
God says, that I have, (A high priest, and a mediator) 125
God says, that I have, (A new covenant) 127
God says, that I have, (Been grafted in to the rich root) 130
God says, that I have, (A new confidence) 135
God says, that I have, (Power over the devil and his demons) ... 137
God says, that I have, (A lawyer, an advocate, with God) 139
God says, that I can, (Do all things in Christ) 141
God says, that I can, (live worry free) 143
God says, that I can, (Receive answers to my prayers) 145
God says, that I can, (Fight the good fight of faith) 146
God says, that I can, (Overcome the world) 149
God says, that I can, (Walk in the spirit) 150
God says, that I can, (Forgive others) 152
God says, that I can, (Cast all my cares upon him) 153
God says, that I can, (Renew my mind, with the word) 155
God says, that I can, (Know his wisdom) 157
God says, that I can, (Find, know, and Do his will) 159
God's will, (Godly identity, New Christian behavior) 163
God's will, His Church, The corporate body of Christ,
    my position? 167

God's will, (His Prerequisite for Bishop, Overseer, Elder) 169
God's will, (His prerequisite for a Deacon) 171
God's will, (His prerequisite, for a minister) 172
God says, that I can, (Be strong like a soldier and an athlete) ... 174
God says, that I can, (be a workman handling
 the word of truth) 176
God says, that I can, (preached the word in season,
 out of season) 178
God says, that I can, (hear his voice through his son) 180
God says I am, God says I have, and God says I can, in Christ 185
The # 1 thing I should do in Christ: (love) 192
The # 2 thing I should do in Christ.
 (Not be a victim of my flesh). 195
The # 3 thing I should do in Christ, is prayer: (Mind) 197
The # 4 thing I should do in Christ, is prayer: (Body) 199
The # 5 thing I should do in Christ, (live the new life) 201
The # 6 thing I should do in Christ, (put off the old man.) 205
The # 7 thing I should do in Christ, (put on the new man.) 207
The # 8 thing I should do in Christ, (walk in the spirit). 210
The # 9 thing I should do in Christ, (Confess our sins, Daily) 212
The # 10 thing I should do in Christ, (Confess our faults). 214
The # 11 thing I should do in Christ, (Be humble) 216
The # 12 thing I should do in Christ, (Not judge a brother) 217
The # 13 thing I should do in Christ, (Not be partial). 219
The # 14 thing that I should do in Christ, (I should mature) ... 221
The # 15 thing I should do in Christ,
 (know why I should mature). 224
The # 16 thing I should do in Christ,
 (Not be friends with the world) 233

The # 17 thing I should do in Christ,
(learn God's economy). 235
The # 18 thing I should do in Christ,
(Discover two kinds of faith) 243
The # 19 thing I should do in Christ,
(discover two kinds of wisdom) 247
The # 20 thing I should do in Christ,
(discover 2 kinds of temptation) 249
The # 22 thing I should do in Christ,
(discover 2 kinds of me) 255
Now the last thing I should do in Christ, (Self-evaluate) 259

ACKNOWLEDGMENT

And as with any major endeavor it takes a great team of people to inspire, to motivat.e, and to be an intricate part in some way shape or form in the production of such a book:

- To which I want to give my sincere thanks for their hard work and untiring commitment:
- To my daughter Annette Arocha, which without her love, unwavering commitment to my life, this book would not have been possible.
- To Pablo M Arocha, who in times of need has proven to be helpful.
- To Mr. Miguel Palacios, for being unafraid to speak his mind, and has beaned a good brother in Christ.
- To Rev. Bobby Rosario, for his love, compassion, caring, and loving spirit.
- To fatih, owner and general manager of Lombardy's rest, Bay side, for his generous contribution and support.
- To Carlos Arocha my younger brother the engineer, and committed hard worker.
- To Marta Canals my sister for her love and devoted hard work.
- To Francisco Arocha a very tough business man, and partial contributor.
- To Mr. Bryant Miller, a brother in Christ, and a partial supporter.
- To miss Susan Weeks for her courage, dedication and support.

- To Mr. Paul and Jan Crouch for their inspiration through Christian television for the last 40 years, through excellent Christian programming.
- To Dr. Mike Murdock for his many inspirational books, and spiritual insight into the holy Bible.
- Mr. Augusto Colorado for his total commitment to us in every area of this project.
- And to the most important person God the Holy Spirit which inspired, revealed, illuminated, and has spoken to my heart, about the great need there is in the body of Christ, to God be the glory.

DEDICATION

The uncompromising truths in this book are dedicated to the many brothers and sisters around the world that are confused, who were not yet transformed by the renewing of their minds, and who are immature in their relationship with God through Christ.

And it is also dedicated to the many brethren who are full of question marks.

- To the one with an extremely low self-value.
- To the one with an extremely low self-worth.
- To the one with an extremely low self-esteem.
- To the one who is constantly up-and-down and confronts depression daily.
- To the one trampled upon theologically.
- To the one that says that Christianity doesn't work.
- To the one who is about to give up on Christianity, or give up on God.
- To the one who is a leader, who will not lead because of a lack of identity?
- To the one rejected by others, and feels that apparently there's no reason to live.
- To the one that feels hopeless, and lonely.
- To the one without direction and doesn't know what to do with his life.
- To the lost and unsaved.
- To the ones who feel inferior to other people.
- To the ones who feel that their leadership capability has been crushed because the failure.

- To the ones who have been told so many times that they will not amount to anything.
- To the ones who are very bright and smart and have been rejected all of their lives because of others envy and jealousy.
- And ultimately to the ones that have been abandoned, forgotten, spoken evil off, whose character has been destroyed by evil gossipers, to justify their sin.

This first edition of the book has never been intended to be explained in storytelling – fashion, but to be shared by individual topics from the book of Genesis to the book of Revelation in order to obtain the completed intent.

And these topics are not presented in their totality, but that the reader may have a completed overview of its original intent.

Its original intent is that every person reading it would discover, understand, and apply what Jesus Christ of Nazareth has already done on the cross in our behalf, his corporate body, his triumphant church, his bride which he is preparing without spot or wrinkle to take up to heaven with him.

And this bride has an identity which he purchased with his precious blood on the cross, of who we are in Christ, what we have in Christ, what we can in Christ, and what we should do in Christ, decreeing with our mouth, and believing with our hearts, what our rights and privileges are, and the power freely given by God.

The identity crisis in the world is at an all-time high in both adolescence as well as adults in the unbelieving world, as well… as Inside the local church.

This book is not intended for debates, nor taken out of order or content, in order to turn it into a debatable issue.

My prayer is that this masterpiece would become a source of faith; a source for identity, a source for acquiring the inheritance bought and paid for by the blood of Jesus Christ on the cross, on the behalf of his redeemed, the triumphant church.

The corporate body of Christ has not yet reached its fullest in stature, fullness in knowledge, and in the power freely given by Jesus Christ himself.

May this book be an inspiration, and instruction in knowledge, in the identity, rights and privileges, and power, that all believers have around the world? May God richly bless you.

"THE CHRISTIAN"
"IDENTITY"
HIS
"RIGHTS AND PRIVILEGES"
AND HIS GOD GIVEN
"POWER"

GOD'S HOLY WORD

In order to start with this wonderful and beautiful masterpiece we have to start with a solid, and a non-movable foundation which is the holy word of Almighty God, the Bible, with its 66 books, 39 books in the Old Testament, and 27 books in the New Testament.

As Jesus said in the Gospel of John chapter 1:1 in the beginning was the word, and the word was with God, and the word was God.

Before anything existed in what we call our planet, a Bible calls it to be in the beginning, was the word, before humans, before animals, before mountains, before rivers, before lakes, before oceans, before anything, was the word, God's holy Scriptures are eternal, just like God himself, he is ever existing, all-powerful, all-knowing, everywhere present.

In Psalms 119:89, 90 Forever, O Lord, Thy word is settled in heaven.

Verse 90, Thy faithfulness continues throughout all generations; thou didst established the earth, and it stands.

This holy word of God is completely settled in heaven, totally unmovable, and unshakable, everything this holy word says we can take it at his core value, believe it, stand on it, decree it, and act upon it, it is settled in heaven and we have an entire Bible full of God's holy word that we can stand on.

God established the earth, his faithfulness continues throughout all generations, because he cannot lie, because he cannot do wrong, he is committed to his written holy word, and when we earthlings read his word, believe his word, act up on his word, his word works because he cannot lie.

He established the earth with 24 hours, 365 days a year, with its four seasons, with the clouds surrounding the earth, with the atmosphere surrounding the earth, with gravity, with beautiful oceans, beautiful mountains, beautiful Springs of water, beautiful animals in the oceans, and human beings all over the earth, close to 7 billion of them, and it stands.

In Psalms 119:105 Thy word is a lamp unto my feet, and a light to my path.

When we hold a lamp in our hands it illuminates our feet regardless of how dark the place is.

And it also says that it is a light to our path in life, it works like a lamp, and it also works like a flashlight, God's holy word keeps us away from darkness in any topic that we will address in life.

In Psalms 119:130 The unfolding of thy words gives light; it gives understanding to the simple.

As we read his holy Scriptures we are enlightened, his unfolding words gives understanding, it gives us the illumination, it gives us revelation, it gives us understanding, and you don't have to be a brain surgeon to understand it, it is designed for the simple.

In Psalms 12:6 The words of the Lord are pure words; As silver tried in a furnace on the earth, refined seven times.

The words of our heavenly father in his Holy Scriptures, they are pure words, honest words, believable sayings, trustworthy, and faithful words that have been tried in an earthly furnace seven times refined.

If God said it, you can believe it, and that settles it, his holy Scriptures are not open for disputes, God is all-knowing, and his word has all the answers.

In Proverbs 4:20, 22 My son, give attention to my words; incline your ear to my sayings.

Verse 21, Do not let them depart from your sight; Keep them in the midst of your heart.

Verse 22, For they are life to those who find them, And health to all their whole body.

Here we see God calling us a son, and his telling us to give attention to his words, to read his words, to meditate on his word, to pay attention when we read his word, and to incline our ears to his sayings, in other words with the heart, not just tickling ears.

And on verse 21 he is encouraging us not to let his holy word depart from our site, but to keep the Holy Scriptures in the midst of our hearts, not just read it with our intellect, but bring it from the mind 16 inches down into the heart.

And the results of his advice because God never says, or encourages us to do something without a benefit, is that they are life to those who find them, and health to all their whole body, my goodness, isn't that glorious, isn't it supernatural, isn't it an overwhelmingly powerful advice, that is just like our God.

In second Timothy 3:16, 17 All Scripture is inspired by God and profitable for teaching, for reproof, for correction, for training in righteousness;

Verse 17, That the man of God may be adequate, equipped for every good work.

All 66 books of God's holy Word the Bible are inspired by God, God used 40 men in the spam of 1600 years, and put his spirit into their body and men became God's pencil, this is how the inspiration of the word came about.

God's holy word was written by the hand of Almighty God through his pencils called man, so he would make it profitable in our lives and teach us everything we will ever need in every area of our lives, it will correct us, reproof us, and train us in righteousness, and right living, so that we who are called men and women of God would be completely adequate, and well-equipped for every good work, aren't you glad that his holy word is all we need to be well-equipped, hallelujah.

GOD THE FATHER

In Genesis chapter 1:1 In the beginning God created the heavens and the earth.

Verse two, And the earth was formless and void, and darkness was over the surface of the deep; and the Spirit of God was moving over the surface of the waters.

Verse three, Then God said, "Let there be light"; and there was light.

Verse four, And God saw that the light was good; and God separated the light from the darkness.

Verse five, And God called the light day, and the darkness he called night, and there was evening and there was morning, one day.

Verse six, Then God said, "Let there be an expanse in the midst of the waters, and let it separate the waters from the waters."

Verse seven, And God made the expanse, and separated the waters which were below the expanse from the waters which were above the expanse; and it was so.

Verse eight, And God called the expanse heaven. And there was evening and there was morning, a second day.

Verse nine, Then God said, "Let the waters below the heavens be gathered into one place, and let the dry land appear"; and it was so.

Verse 10, And God called the dry land Earth, and the gathering of the waters he called seas; and God saw that it was good.

Verse 11, Then God said, "Let the earth sprout vegetation, plants yielding seed, and fruit trees bearing fruit after their kind, with seed in them, on the earth"; and it was so.

Verse 12, And the earth brought forth vegetation, plants yielding seed after their kind, and trees bearing fruit, with seed in them, after their kind; and God saw that it was good.

Verse 13, And there was evening and there was morning, a third day.

Verse 14, And God said, "Let there be lights in the expanse of the heavens to separate the day from the night, and let them be for signs, and for seasons, and for days and years;

Verse 15, and let them be for lights in the expanse of the heavens to give light on the earth"; and it was so.

Verse 16, And God made the two great lights, the greater light to govern the day, and the lesser light to govern the night; he made the stars also.

Verse 17, And God placed them in the expanse of the heavens to give light on the earth,

Verse 18, and to govern the day and the night, and to separate the light from the darkness; and God saw that it was good.

Verse 19, And there was evening and there was morning, a fourth day.

Verse 20, And God said, "Let the waters teem with swarms of living creatures, and let birds fly above the earth in the open expanse of the heavens."

Verse 21, When God created the great sea monsters, and every living creature that moves, with which the waters swarmed after their kind, and every winged bird after its kind; and God saw that it was good.

Verse 22, And God blessed them, saying, "Be fruitful and multiply, and fill the waters in the seas, and let the birds multiply on the earth."

Verse 23, And there was evening and there was morning, a fifth day.

Verse 24, Then God said, "Let the earth bring forth living creatures after their kind: cattle and creeping things and beast of the earth after their kind"; and it was so.

Verse 25, And God made the beast of the earth after their kind, and the cattle after their kind, and everything that creeps on the ground after its kind; and God saw that it was good.

Verse 26, Then God said, "Let us make man in our image, according to our likeness; and let them rule over the fish of the sea and over the birds of the sky and over the cattle and over all the earth, and over every creeping thing that creeps on the earth,"

Verse 27, And God created man in his own image, in the image of God he created him; male and female he created them.

Verse 28, And God blessed them; and God said to them, "Be fruitful and multiply, and fill the earth, and subdue it; and rule over the fish of the sea and over the birds of the sky, and over every living thing that moves on the earth."

Verse 29, Then God said, "Behold, I have given you every plant yielding seed that is on the surface of all the earth, and every tree which has fruit yielding seed; it shall be food for you;

Verse 30 and to every beast of the earth and to every bird of the sky, I have given every green plant for food"; and it was so.

Verse 31, And God so all that he had made, and behold, it was very good. And there was evening and there was morning, the sixth day.

Now the first thing we want to see here is that God the father is the creator of everything that exists, we are the byproduct of a God who is a Creator, we're not the byproduct of a big bang theory, if you notice from verse 1 to verse 31 God created the earth separated the waters from the dry land, and called the water seas, and called the dry land Earth, he made every creeping animals on the earth, and every fowl of the air, every animal in the seas, but the beautiful part of it is, he said plants yielding seed after their kind, after their kind, after their kind, the reason why I am repeating myself is so that you the reader may understand that animals, plants, and human beings did not evolve, they were all created after their kind.

God the creator, not Darwin's evolutionary system, but God the creator created the plants, animals in the ocean, animals on the earth, animals in the air, after their kind.

Now before we go on, you are definitely reading the creation theory, by the hand of a master creator, who had an original intent for creating everything, which he did, and he put it all inside the garden.

The method that God used in order to create everything was his precious Holy Spirit carrying out the tasks spoken by his mouth, God would say let there be, and it was the Holy Spirit who would carry out every spoken word.

There's something very interesting here on verse 49, but I would like for you to also consider, when he said let us, in our image, in our likeness.

When God uses the word let us, when God uses the word in our image, and when God uses the word in our likeness, it is very obvious that there was somebody else with him in the beginning, and we read it in the beginning of this book.

We don't want to repeat ourselves what I want to bring to your remembrance, that in the gospel of John chapter 1:1 it says in the beginning was the word, and the word was with God, and the word was God, and on verse 14, we read, and the word became flesh, and dwelt among us, and we beheld his glory, glory as of the only begotten from the father, full of grace and truth.

So when God said let us, in our image, according to our likeness, he was referring to Jesus Christ of Nazareth, the only begotten of the father full of grace and truth, so let's get this straight now before anything ever existed God the father existed, Jesus the son existed, God the Holy Spirit existed, and the word of Almighty God existed, so it is safe to say that when we read the holy Scriptures we are reading the inspired, word, that became flesh.

I would also like to bring to your attention where it said that God blessed them, and said to them to be fruitful and multiply, and to fill the earth, and subdue it, and to have dominion, over the fish in the sea, over every fowl of the air, and every living thing on the earth.

Our heavenly father, did not only make us in his image and likeness, by making us an eternal soul, breathing into our nostrils the breath of life and making us a living soul, but he also gave us a commission, a task, a job to fulfill, we were to subdue the earth, we were to replenish the earth, we were to have dominion over the earth, and over the fish in the sea, over the birds in the sky, and over every living thing on the earth.

God never does anything, or creates anyone, without a purpose, everything spoken into existence, and carried out by the Holy Spirit of God, had a divined purpose, and a very creative reason behind it, our heavenly father is the greatest master builder, and creator, of everything that exists, including us. We were created to have dominion, subdue the earth, and rule over every living thing that moves over the earth.

In other words we were to Lord over everything on this planet, becoming the Stewarts of it.

In Genesis chapter 2:1 Thus the heavens and the earth were completed, and all their hosts.

Verse two, And by the seventh day God completed his work which he had done; and he rested on the seventh day from all his work which he had done.

Verse three, Then God blessed the seventh day and sanctified it, because in it he rested from all his work which God had created and made.

And on verse seven, the Lord God formed man out of the dust of the ground and breathed into his nostrils the breath of life; and man became a living being.

Verse eight, And the Lord God planted a garden toward the east, in Eden; and there he placed the man whom he had formed.

Verse 15, The Lord God took the man and put him into the Garden of Eden to cultivate and keep it.

Verse 16, On the Lord God commanded the man, saying, "From any tree of the garden you may eat freely;

Verse 17, but from the tree of the knowledge of good and evil you shall not eat, for in that day that you eat from it you shall surely die."

Verse 18, Then the Lord God said, "Is not good for man to be alone; I will make him a helper suitable for him,"

Verse 19, Out of the ground the Lord God formed every beast of the field and every bird of the sky, and brought them to the man to see what he would call them; and whatsoever the man called the living creature, that was its name.

Verse 20, And the man gave names to all the cattle, and to all the birds of the sky, and to every beast of the field, but for Adam there was not found a helper suitable for him.

As we can see here the purpose for God's creation was to cultivate the garden of Eden and keep it, and God gives man the first instruction, he commands the man that he could eat from all the trees in the garden, but from the tree of knowledge of good and evil you shall not eat thereof, and he explains to man the consequence of the sin of omission, you shall surely die, God did not want men to die, and having a sinful fallen nature.

Then God says it is not good for man to be alone, for those of you out there that are divorced, and think that you don't need a partner to navigate through life, God said it is not good for man to be alone, and then he said I will make him helper, suitable for him.

On verse 19 notice how God made all the animals of the earth, and notice how he brought them to Adam to see what he would call them, that is very interesting, and whatever Adam called them that was its name.

We see a God of creation, we see a God of purpose, we see a God of missions, we see the creation of everything, the purpose behind the creation, we see God providing man a helper to fulfill his calling, his help meet someone suitable for him.

Verse 21, The Lord God Caused a Deep Sleep to Fall upon the Man, and He Slept; Then He Took One of His Ribs, and Closed up the Flesh at That Place.

Verse 22, And the Lord God fashioned into a woman the rib which he had taken from man, and brought her to the man.

Verse 23, And the man said, "This is now bone of my bones, And flesh of my flesh; she shall be called woman, because she was taken out of man."

Verse 24, For this cause a man shall leave his father and his mother, and shall cleave to his wife; and they shall become one flesh.

Verse 25, And the man and his wife were both naked and were not ashamed.

In chapter 3:1 Now the serpent was more crafty than any beast of the field which the Lord God had made. And he said to the woman, "indeed, has God said, 'You shall not eat from any tree of the garden'?"

Verse two, And the woman said to the serpent, "From the fruit of the trees of the garden we may eat;

Verse three, but from the fruit of the tree which is in the middle of the garden, God has said, 'You shall not eat from it or touch it, lest you die.'

Verse four, And the serpent said to the woman, "You surely shall not die!

Verse five, "For God knows that in the day you eat from it your eyes will be opened, and you will be like God, knowing good and evil."

Verse six, When the woman saw that the tree was good for food, and that it was a delight to the eyes, and that the tree was desirable to make one wise, she took from its fruit and ate; and she gave also unto her husband with her, and he ate.

Let's start noticing some important things here, the woman is formed by the left rib of the male, not by a bone from his head so that she will not Lord over him, nor was she formed from a bone out of his feet, so that he will not step all over her, but From the left rib of man, and to this day you can ask a medical doctor that males have one less rib on their left side than female. Know why from the left rib? Because that is where the heart is, women should be man's helper, completer, a complementary to his original task.

Women are equal to men, but with a different role to play within the marriage, women was not made for war, but to be one with her man, complete him, and help him, in his role in life, and together becoming one flesh replenishing the earth.

Now in heaven God had formed three major ark Angels, Michael, Gabriel, and Lucifer.

Now when the Bible says the serpent was craftier than any beast of the field, it was because Lucifer the Ark Angel which was created by God, and was thrown out of heaven, and a third of God's created angels followed Lucifer. At this time He had already entered the serpent, and spoke through the serpent, and in so doing deceived the woman, every time the enemy wants to deceive God's people, he starts by a question, has God said.

On verse six when the woman saw that the tree was good for food, and that it was a delight to the eyes, and that the tree was desirable to make one wise, she took from the fruit and ate, and she also gave some to her husband and he ate, and this is where trouble

begun. When the sin of omission, which is forgetfulness, carelessness, and disobedience, enters your eye gate, the sin of commission, which is the act of doing what, is wrong, sets in and we fall.

This is where the judgment of God begins, in the sin of omission, and the sin of commission, and a loving heavenly father, Master creator, a God of love, a God of compassion, mercy, understanding, tenderness, gentleness, cannot, and will not deal with man's disobedience in the area of omission and commission, God has two pass judgments.

And in Genesis chapter 3:14,19 And the Lord God said to the serpent, "Because you have done this, cursed are you more than all cattle, and more than every beast of the field; on your belly shall you go, and dust shall you eat all the days of your life;

Verse 15, And I will put enmity between you and the woman, and between your seed and her seed; He shall bruise you on the head, and you shall bruise him on the heel."

On verse 15 we see a loving tender heavenly father making his first covenant with man, of what he was going to do through Jesus Christ of Nazareth under the new dispensation of grace, the new covenant established with better promises.

Verse 16, To the woman he said, "I will greatly multiply your pain in childbirth, in pain you shall bring forth children; yet your desire shall be for your husband, and he shall rule over you."

Verse 17, Then to Adam he said, "Because you have listened to the voice of your wife, and have eaten from the tree about which I commanded you, saying, 'You shall not eat from it'; Cursed is the ground because of you; and in toil you shall eat of it all the days of your life.

Verse 18, "Both thorns and thistles it shall grow for you; and you shall eat the plants of the field;

Verse 19, by the sweat of your face you shall eat bread, till you return to the ground, because from it you were taken; for you are dust, and to dust you shall return."

Verse 20, Now the man called his wife's name Eve, because she was the mother of all the living.

Verse 21, And the Lord God made garments of skin for Adam and his wife, and closed them.

Verse 22, Then the Lord God said, "Behold, the man has become like one of us, knowing good and evil; and now, lest he stretched out his hand, and take also from the tree of life, and eat, and live forever"-

Verse 23, therefore the Lord God sent him out from the Garden of Eden, to cultivate the ground from which he was taken.

Verse 24, So he drove the man out; and at the east of the garden of Eden he stationed the cherubim, and the flaming sword which turned every direction, to guard the way to the tree of life.

And in chapter 4:1, 14 we see the man and woman get together and had two children Cain and Abel, and Abel found grace in the sight of God, and Cain was jealous of it, and we know the whole story, how Cain slew Abel because of the jealousy that he had of his brother, he became a deceiver, he became a con artist, he became a liar, he became a murderer.

This is where all the evil on this earth came from, the children of Adam and Eve, after Abel died Cain went North East and did his life, and Adam and Eve were together one more time and had another child by the name set, which all of the descendants came from up until the Ark of Noah, where God had to destroy the earth with a flood, and the children of Noah were the ones that replenished the earth where we all came out of.

Now let us recap God the father, a spirit being creator of the heavens and the earth the, sun the moon and the stars, created all the creatures inside the seas, created all the flying birds, created all the cattle and every living creature, then he forms his masterpiece the human race, and as you very well may read, it is sin, willful disobedience, a fallen sinful nature, that totally alienates us from God, God's original intent was good and perfect and to make as the Lord of this earth.

God's main name is Jehovah, In Exodus chapter 3:14 (I AM THAT I AM) he said to Moses. In order to understand our heavenly father we must understand what his names mean.

- Jehovah-Jireh the (Lord our provider) this is found in Genesis chapter 22:14.
- Jehovah-Rafa the (Lord our healer) this is found in Exodus chapter 15:26.
- Jehovah-nisi the (Lord my standard) this is found in Exodus chapter 17:15.
- Jehovah-M'-kaddesh the (Lord who sanctifies) this is found in Leviticus chapter 20:8.

- Jehovah-Sabaoth the (Lord of the armies) this is found in first Samuel 1:3.
- Jehovah- shalom the (Lord our peace) this is found in judges chapter 6:24.
- Jehovah-Roi the (Lord is my shepherd) this is found in the Psalms chapter 23:1.
- Jehovah-Tsid Kenu the (Lord our righteousness) this is found in Jeremiah chapter 23:6.
- Jehovah- Shamma the (Lord is there) this is found in Ezekiel chapter 48:35.

Just by the names of our heavenly father we can bank the rest of our lives, because his words, his names, his covenants, and his dispensations do not change.

There's a lot more that could be said about our father Jehovah God the creator, which we will address later on, but for now you have a comprehensive amount of knowledge based on what you read, of what our heavenly father is, has done, and continually do in our behalf.

Our heavenly father, is a God of covenant's, and in Genesis chapter 9:9, 17 we see how God made a covenant with Noah, that he would never destroy the human race ever again with water, and every time it rains we look up in the sky and we see the rainbow, it should always remind us, that God is a never changing God, he keeps his word, he is faithful to his word, and he doesn't go back on his word, just like all human beings do, aren't you glad that you can take him at his word.

Our God is an everlasting heavenly father, all-powerful, everywhere present, and all-knowing, who is also a personal and intimate heavenly father, and we will talk more about that further on.

GOD'S 7 COVENANT

In Genesis chapter 15:18 God made a covenant with Abraham, and his descendants.

And in Genesis chapter 21:13, 21 God makes a covenant with the descendants of Ishmael, the same God of Abraham Isaac and Jacob, and he should be there God.

In Deuteronomy chapter 5:2, 3 God made a covenant with Moses and the children of Israel.

In second Samuel's chapter 23:5 God made everlasting covenant with David.

In Hebrews chapter 8:1, 13 God makes an everlasting covenant with people throughout the world, who believe in the Lord Jesus Christ through the shed blood.

Genesis 3: 15 Genesis 9:9, 17 Genesis 15:18 Genesis 21:13, 21 Deuteronomy 5:2,3

Second Samuel's 23,5 and Hebrews chapter 8:1, 13.

These are the seven covenants, commitments, method in which God committed his word to people to be faithful, to be loyal, and to be committed, our heavenly father has a holy and written word which he is committed to perform it in our lives, and is not like a human being that changes his mind every time things don't go their way.

Aren't you glad, aren't you happy, aren't you secured in this eternal constitution, God's old and New Testament, with so many liars, with so many jokers, with so many deceivers, that say something and do something different, it is truly refreshing to know that our heavenly father is worthy of our full faith in his written holy word, an all-powerful, all-knowing, and everywhere present God, he can be believed. This is why it's so important to make God's holy word our personal love letter, and read it for ourselves.

GOD'S OLD TESTAMENT

Now the Bible has 66 books, 39 books in the Old Testament, 27 books in the New Testament, and in the Old Testament the first 39 books of the Bible there are (six covenants) and (five dispensations). Our last covenant is the seventh covenant which God made with the people through Jesus Christ found in the New Testament, the Hebrews chapter 8:1, 13. Now this better covenant that is found in the New Testament, with better promises, through a once and for all sacrificed Lamb, it's also called the New Testament, which is the dispensation of grace, number six, God's goodness towards humanity, through faith in Jesus Christ our Lord. Also the first 5 books of the Old Testament are called the Pentateuch or the books of the law, the next 12 books are considered the history books, while the fallowing 5 are considered the poetry books, the fallowing 5 are considered the Major Prophets, and the last 12 are the Minor Prophets. For a total of 39 books in all.

GOD'S 7 DISPENSATIONS

Number One, is called the dispensation of innocence and it's found in Genesis 1:28.

Number two, is called the dispensation of conscience and is found in Genesis 3:7.

Number three, is called the dispensation of human government and is found in Genesis 8:20.

Number four, is called the dispensation of the promise and is found in Genesis 12:1 and Romans 4:13.

Number five, is called the dispensation of law and is founding Exodus 19:8 and Matthew's 5:17.

Number six, is called the dispensation of grace and is found in the gospel of John 1:17 and Romans 6:14.

Number seven, is called the dispensation of the millennial reign of Christ and is found in Ephesians chapter 1:10 and revelations chapter 20:4,5.

I looked up the word dispensation in Webster's comprehensive dictionary and I found six very interesting terms to that word and I quote.

Number one, the act of dispensing; a dealing out; distribution.

Number two, that which is bestowed on or appointed to one from a higher power.

Number three, The Devine arrangement and administration of the affairs of the world: the dispensation of Providence.

Number four, a specific plan: a special dispensation of nature.

Number five, Special exception granted from the requirements of a law, rule, or obligation.

Number six, Theol. One of the several systems or bodies of law in which at different times and God has revealed his mind and will to man, or the continued state of things resulting from the operation of one of these systems: the Mosaic dispensation; also, the period during which a particular revelation of God's mind and will has been directly operative on mankind: during the Christian dispensation.

Now the six interpretation of the word dispensation, correlates with exactly what you have been reading about God the father, how he dispensed, he dealt with, and distributed animals and humans around the world, the first one was, the dispensation of innocence, the second one was, the dispensation of conscience man had already sinned, the third had to be the dispensation of government, that man had to have, with Rules and regulations to govern himself by, then the fourth dispensation of promise, God's promise to human beings to bless them and give them lands and the messiah, then the fifth dispensation of law, with the 10 Commandments, then because men broke every one of the 10 Commandments, then the six, God establishes the dispensation of grace, the unmerited favor attributed to man by faith in the ultimate sacrificed Lamb Jesus Christ of Nazareth, and then number seven, the dispensation which is the millennial reign of Christ, where there will be physical earthly government in Israel with Jesus Christ sitting on the throne.

His 24 elders by his side, and all of the Saints that were raptured passed through the judgment seat of Christ, went to the marriage supper of the Lamb, and then came to the battle of Armageddon, and established the seventh dispensation, more on this dispensation later.

GOD'S NEW TESTAMENT: A DISPENSATION OF GRACE

The New Testament has 27 books, of which the first 4 are called the Gospels, the gospel of Matthew's, the gospel of Mark, the gospel of Luke, and the gospel of John.

Then comes the book of acts, which is considered the Acts of the Apostles, and the formation of the original church, called the history book.

The nine epistles that the apostle Paul wrote, starting with the letter to the Roman church, first and second Corinthians, letter to the town of Corinth.

Then the epistle to the Galatians, then the epistle to the Ephesians, then the epistle to the Philippians, to the Colossians, first and second Thessalonians, for a total of nine epistles.

Then the apostle Paul wrote his epistles to his friends, first and second Timothy, the epistle to Titus, and the epistle to Philemon.

Then came the letter to the Hebrews, which talked about the difference between law and grace, then came the general epistles, which include the epistle of James, first and second Peter, first second and third John, the epistle of Jude, and the last book of the Bible which is the book of revelations.

These are all the 27 books of the new covenant, dispensation of the unmerited favor of God, through Jesus Christ our Lord, where we get our identity, writes and privileges, our God-given power, and destiny.

It is in this number six Christian dispensation of grace, which is the unmerited favor of God bestowed upon humanity, is where we need to deal with in this whole entire teaching. What has transpired on the cross on the behalf of human beings, the gift of substitution, in order to pardon, the gift of eternal life, the complete redemption for human beings, the empowering of humans to live their Christian life, the established church of the lord Jesus Christ, their millennial reign with Christ, and their life for all eternity.

When the Bible says to the fullness of time, it is from the birth of Jesus Christ until today, the summing up of the things in Christ, in the heavens and on the earth.

It is vitally important to understand what we are about to read from now on. God has revealed, the administration of his mystery that was hidden in God, and the manifold wisdom to us his church, and that we may make it known through the church to the rulers and authorities in heavenly places, which was according to his eternal purpose which he carried out in Jesus Christ our Lord. Very Powerful Statement, let's read up.

In Ephesians chapter 1: 10, Suitable to the fullness of times, but it's, the summing up of all things in Christ, things in the heavens and things up on the earth.

On Ephesians 3:9 and to bring to light what is the administration of the mystery which for ages has been hidden in God, who created all things;

Verse 10, in order that the manifold wisdom of God might now be made known through the church to the rulers of the authorities in the heavenly places.

Verse 11, This was in accordance with the eternal purpose which he had carried out in Christ Jesus our Lord.

This manifold wisdom has been manifested in us through Jesus Christ our Lord.

In the gospel of Mark chapter 16:15, 18 And he said to them, "Go into all the world and preach the gospel to all creation.

Verse 16, "He who has believed and has been baptized shall be saved; but he who has disbelieved shall be condemned.

Verse 17, "And these signs will accompany those who have believed: in my name they will cast out demons, they will speak with new tongues;

Verse 18, they will pick up serpents, and if they drink any deadly poison, it shall not hurt them; they will lay hands on the sick, and they will recover."

The word gospel is good news, unmerited favor, God's total redemptive power, and this is what we will be addressing throughout this book. He would never give us a commission to fulfill without empowering us to fulfill it, and this is what we will discover further on in this book.

GOD THE SON

In the gospel of John chapter 1:1 it says in the beginning was the word, and the word was with God, and the word was God.

Verse 14, And the word became flesh, and dwelt among us, and we beheld his glory, glory as of the only begotten from the father, full of grace and truth.

Jesus Christ of Nazareth as we read in previous passages was in the beginning with the father, his holy word was also in the beginning, and the father was also in the beginning, and the Holy Spirit was also in the beginning.

So every time we read the holy word of God, he is speaking to us through his son Jesus Christ, in the gospel of Matthew's chapter 1:21,23 "And she will bear a son; and you shall call his name Jesus, for it is he who will save his people from their sins."

Verse 22, Now all this took place that what was spoken by the Lord through the prophet might be fulfilled saying,

Verse 23, "Behold, the virgin shall be with child, and shall bear a son, and they shall call his name Emmanuelle," which translated means, "God with us."

God the father took upon himself flesh, and became God the son, which is what we want to address before we move on.

The name Jesus means Savior, he came to save us, he came to redeem us, he came to destroy the works of the devil in our lives, he came to save us from our sin, he came to snatch us out from the grip of hell, and a sinful nature that we were born with, which is the sinful nature which we inherited through Adam and Eve in the garden, no human being can escape from his sinful nature, we were all conceived in the womb of our mothers in sin.

The alienated and rebellious state of human beings, is clearly seen in the newborn babe's when they start walking; they rebel against all established authority, and are stubborn, this fallen state is something we are born with.

In the gospel of John chapter 1:2 He was in the beginning with God.

Verse three, all things came into being by him, and apart from him nothing came into being that has come into being.

Verse four, in him was life, and the life was the light of men.

Verse five, and the light shines in the darkness, and the darkness did not comprehend it.

Verse nine, There was that true light which, coming into the world, enlightens every man.

Verse 10, He was in the world, and the world was made through him, and the world did not know him.

Verse 11, He came to his own, and those who were his own did not receive him.

Verse 12, But as many as received him, to them gave he the right to become children of God, even to those who believe in his name,

Verse 13, who were born not of blood, nor of the will of the flesh, nor of the will of man, but of God.

Let's recap A little bit here, Jesus, = Savior from our sin, Emmanuelle God with us.

Who was in the beginning with God, and everything we see created came into being by him, and apart from him nothing came into being.

Everyrhing created came into being by Jesus Christ.

In him was life, and the life was the light of men, Jesus inside of us illuminate us from the inside and out, that is why the gospel of Matthew's chapter 5:14 Jesus said that we are the light of the world. A city set on a hill cannot be hidden.

Jesus is also called the light that enlightens humanity, and this beautiful light shines in darkness, and the darkness comprehended it not.

He was in the world, and the world was made by him, and the world knew him not, he came to the Jewish people, and his own received him not, but as many as received him, to them gave he the right to become children of God, even to those who believe on his name.

These are the purposes as to why God came in the person of Jesus Christ, everything we have just read is exactly what happens in our lives, when we acknowledge our sin, and receive Jesus Christ as our Savior and Lord, he comes into our lives and fills our void and takes up residence within us, and we become a born again Christian.

In the gospel of John chapter 14:9, 11 Jesus said to him, "Have I been so long with you, and yet you have not come to know me,

Philip? He who has seen me has seen the father; how do you say, Show us the father?

Verse 10, "To you not believe that I am in the father, and the father is in me? The words that I say to you I do not speak of my own initiative, but the father abiding in me does his works.

Verse 11, "Believe me that I am in the father, and the father in me; otherwise believe on account of the works themselves.

Verse 12, "Truly, truly, I say to you, he who believes in me, the works that I do shall he do also; and greater works than these shall he do; because I go to the father.

God the son was manifested with a particular purpose in mind, that is to establish the new covenant, to redeemed the fallen human race, to pay the ultimate price once and for all, for without the shedding of his innocent blood there is no remission for sin.

In second Corinthians chapter 5:19 namely, that God was in Christ reconciling the world to himself, not counting their trespasses against them, and he has committed to us the word of reconciliation.

The mission of God in the person of Jesus Christ is clear, to purchase, to reconcile, to unite human beings with him, through the shedding of his own blood on the cross, for the establishment of communion and fellowship once again, lost in the garden.

Jesus Christ of Nazareth did not come into the world to establish a human government, under the dispensation of grace, but as a sacrificed Lamb to redeem fallen mankind, and this is why the Jewish people did not understand his mission, that is why he came to his own and his own received him not, the Jewish Messiah came to the Jewish people and they received him not, but as many as received him, to them gave he the right to become children of God. God in Christ reconciling the world to himself, not counting their trespasses against them.

There are thousands of things that God the father, in the person of Jesus Christ came to do on the Cross, primarily to establish fellowship and common union with human beings.

Jesus Christ is not a religion, Jesus Christ is God in person, Jesus Christ is Emmanuelle, Jesus Christ is a sacrificed Lamb, Jesus Christ is a mediator, Jesus Christ's holy blood is the new covenant, with better promises, Jesus Christ is the word incarnate, Jesus Christ is the high priest, and Jesus Christ is now our heavenly lawyer, seated at the right hand of the father, and without faith in his total sacrificial death burial and resurrection, there is definitely no remission for sin.

GOD THE HOLLY SPIRIT

The Holy Spirit is the third person of the holy Trinity, in the gospel of Matthew's chapter 28:19 "Go therefore and make disciples of all nations, baptizing them in the name of the father and the son and the Holy Spirit,

Verse 20, teaching them to observe all that I have commanded you; and low, I am with you always, even to the end of the age."

So in understanding the Holy Spirit, we have got to understand this is a commission that Jesus Christ himself gave us, and in every generation to come if he tarries.

In order to disciple an entire nation we must preach the gospel to them, the full gospel, and then as they get saved, we need to baptize them in the name of the father, and of the son, and of the Holy Spirit, and then we need to teach them and educate them, to observe all of the teachings that Jesus himself commanded us to observe.

In Genesis chapter 1:2 we see how the spirit of God was moving over the surface of the waters, it is that same Holy Spirit that will seal and baptize us for the necessary fulfillment of the commission.

In second Corinthians chapter 13:14 The grace of the Lord Jesus Christ, and the love of God, and the fellowship of the Holy Spirit, be with you all. (Fellowship with the Holy Spirit is exactly what we all need in today's day and age.)

Precious Holy Spirit convicts us of sin in the gospel of John chapter 16:8 "And he, when he comes, will convict the world concerning sin, and righteousness, and judgment;

Verse nine, concerning sin, because they do not believe in me;

Verse 10, and concerning righteousness, because I go to the father, and you will no longer behold me;

Verse 11, and concerning judgment, because the ruler of this world has been judged.

Is important to understand that it is the power of the Holy Spirit that convicts the sinner that he needs a Savior, it is only through that conviction that the sinner repents.

The precious Holy Spirit resides within the Christian, in the gospel of John chapter 14:17 that is the spirit of truth, whom the world cannot receive, because it does not behold him or know him, but you know him because he abides with you, and will be in you.

Please remember the word in you, and abides with you.

It was the Holy Spirit who inspired the word of Almighty God, and it is the Holy Spirit who speaks to our hearts through the holy Scriptures, in the book of acts chapter 1:16 "Brethren, the Scripture had to be fulfilled, which the Holy Spirit foretold by the mouth of David concerning Judas, who became a guide to those who arrested Jesus.

In second Peter chapter 1:21 for no prophecy was ever made by an act of human will, but men moved by the Holy Spirit spoke from God.

Throughout Scriptures we see that the Holy Spirit moved to carry out the commands, the prophecies, and the decrees directly from God through men.

In the epistle of Paul to second Timothy chapter 3:16 All Scripture is inspired by God and profitable for teaching, for reproof, for correction, for training in righteousness;

Verse 17, that the man of God may be adequate, equipped for every good work.

When the Scripture says, that all Scriptures are inspired by God, God the Holy Spirit breathed into human beings and they were moved as the spirit told them what to write. The Bible contains 66 books written by 40 men in a span of about 1600 years without any contradiction, because of the inspiration of the Holy Spirit, so when Paul says in the epistle to Timothy that all Scripture is inspired by God, he was not a physical God who wrote it, but the spirit of God moving through his earthly pencils, the men.

Thank God his precious Holy Spirit is the same yesterday today and forever, God does not change, he is all-powerful, he is all knowing, he is everywhere present, and the only way he can be everywhere present at the same time, is by his Holy Spirit.

In the epistle of Paul to the Roman church chapter 8:26 And in the same way the Spirit also helps our weakness; for we do not know how to pray as we should, but the spirit himself intercedes for us with groaning's too deep for words;

Verse 27, and he searches the hearts knows what the mind of the spirit is, because he intercedes for the saints according to the will of God.

It is the Holy Spirit that helps us, when we are down and out and week, and our minds are confused and we don't know how to pray, but when we open our hearts to the father and we come to him in Jesus name, then the holy spirit within us cries Abba father, and we start the fellowship with the precious Holy Spirit, and God who is the spirit will response to our immediate need, hallelujah.

In first Corinthians chapter 12:11 But one and the same spirit works all these things, God distributing to each one individually just as he wills.

Here we see the Holy Spirit counting on, with attributes that of a personality, he has a will, and he does as he wills.

In Romans chapter 8:27 and he who searches the hearts knows what the mind of the Spirit is, because he intercedes for the saints according to the will of God.

In this passage of Scripture's we see the Holy Spirit having a mind of his own, and interceding for the saints according to the will of God.

That is why it's so important for all of us to be filled with the Holy Spirit, he has a mind of his own and he intercedes for us according to the will of the father.

In this other chapter and verse we will see the Holy Spirit, having a thought life, having knowledge, and speaking words.

In first Corinthians chapter 2:10, 13 For to us Revealed them through the spirit; for the Spirit searches all things, even the depths of God.

Verse 11, For who among men knows the thoughts of a man except the spirit of the man, which is in him? Even so the thoughts of God no one knows except the spirit of God,

Verse 13, which things we also speak, not in words taught by human wisdom, but in those taught by the Spirit, combining spiritual thoughts with spiritual words.

In order to know the thoughts of God, in order to know the perfect spiritual will of God for man, we must be baptized in the Holy Spirit, every born-again Christian has a spiritual rebirth, he is a new creation, but if he has not had a baptism of the Holy Spirit, he is missing out on the best of God.

In the epistle of Paul to the church in Rome, Romans 15: 30 Now I urge you, brethren, by our Lord Jesus Christ and by the love of the Spirit, to strive together with me in your prayers to God for me.

Here we see is the Holy Spirit who puts sufficient love within the human heart, after we received the baptism, in order to love human beings, he is the giver of love, after all, the fruit of the Holy Spirit is love.

In these next passages the Holy Spirit can be treated as a person, can be tempted, and lied to.

In the acts of the apostles chapter 5:3,4 But Peter said, "Ananias, why has Satan filled your heart to lie to the Holy Spirit, and to keep back some of the price of the land?

Verse four, "While it remained unsold, did it not remain your own?

And after it was sold, was it not under your control? You have not lied to men, but to God."

When we are baptized in the Holy Spirit, one of the gifts of the Holy Spirit is discernment of spirits, here we see the apostle Peter discerning the lie, the deception, and the temptation that Ananias had brought upon the Holy Spirit, the apostle Peter was baptized with the Holy Spirit, which is also God, that is why he said you have not lied to men, but to God, the Holy Spirit is God.

That is why in some circles when they say that the Holy Spirit baptism was only for the time of the apostles, then God must have seized to exist at that time, thereby destroying his attributes, God is all-powerful, God is all-knowing, God everywhere present, how can the baptism of the Holy Spirit ceased to exist, when God and the Holy Spirit are one and the same.

In acts chapter 7:51 "You men who are stiff- necked and uncircumcised in your heart and ears are always resisting the Holy Spirit; you are doing just as your fathers did.

Here we see that the people that were uncircumcised in heart and ears were constantly resisting, the revelation, the power, and the knowledge of the Holy Spirit, isn't that like some of us today who are constantly resisting the gentleness of the Holy Spirit, his precious revelations, his precious anointing, his precious power, the Holy Spirit is God. And by rejecting the move of the Holy Spirit in our lives we are resisting him who is God.

In the epistle of Paul to the Ephesians chapter 4:30 And do not grieve the Holy Spirit of God, by whom you were sealed for the day of redemption.

In this passage of Scripture we see how the Holy Spirit can be grieved, when we don't believe he is for today, when we resist him, you are grieving him.

In the gospel of Matthew's chapter 12:31 "Therefore I say to you, any sin and blasphemy shall be forgiven men, but blasphemy against the Spirit shall not be forgiven.

Verse 32, "And whoever shall speak a word against the Son of Man, it shall be forgiven him; but whoever shall speak against the Holy Spirit, it shall not be forgiven him, either in this age, or in the age to come.

So when we attribute the gifts of the Holy Spirit, the fruit of the Holy Spirit, to the workings of the devil, that is considered blasphemy against the Holy Spirit, we must be very careful that if we haven't experienced the baptism of the Holy Spirit, not to attribute his gifts and fruits to the workings of the enemy, the devil does not love human beings.

God the Holy Spirit is very much alive and well, and I have personally received the baptism in the Holy Spirit, with the gifts, and the fruit operating in my life, thereby flooding my soul with an unconditional agape love for human beings, and their need for God.

God the Holy Spirit is alive and well, and all he is waiting for is for us to raise our arms to the sky, and say Abba father, I worship you, I magnify you, I give you praise and adoration, for you are worthy heavenly father, you are worthy heavenly father, and I worship you in spirit and in truth, please heavenly father, by the manifestation of the Holy Spirit, fill me with the third person of the holy Trinity in my life, I want to receive the baptism in the Holy Spirit now, come into my heart precious Holy Spirit, I surrender my intellect, I surrender all of my question marks? And I worship you, God the Holy Spirit you are welcomed in my house, in my room, in my life, you are welcomed in every area of my life, you said in your word that if I believed in the Lord Jesus Christ, that out of my belly shall flow rivers of living waters, I want that experience right now Lord in Jesus holy name I pray amen.

My brother and my sister if you raise both of your arms up to the sky, and you ask The Holy Spirit to fill you he will, and in spite that perhaps you didn't sense as much as you would like, please try doing this prayer over and over again, and I can assure you buy the authority of the holy word of God, his precious Holy Spirit will manifest himself, hallelujah.

If you have blasphemed the Holy Spirit, tell God that you repent from that, and that you are sorry, and to cleanse you, and to wash you with the precious blood of Jesus, and that you desire fellowship with the Holy Spirit, and immediately you will be cleansed, and delivered in Jesus name, amen.

In first Corinthians chapter 12:2, 11 You know that when you were pagans, you were led astray to the dumb idols, however you were led.

Verse three, Therefore I make known to you, that no one speaking by the Spirit of God says, "Jesus is accursed"; and no one can say, "Jesus is Lord," except by the Holy Spirit.

Here we see that when we all were pagans we were still led by a spirit to dumb idols, and that no one by that same spirit can say Jesus is Lord.

It Is by God the Holy Spirit in our hearts that we call Jesus Lord, and it is that same spirit that reveals all of the teachings of Jesus Christ in our lives, so when we are saved we are Holy Spirit sealed, Ephesians 4:13 but then comes the manifestation, or the baptism of the Holy Spirit with the gifts that we are about to read in these next verses.

Verse four, Now there are varieties of gifts, but the same spirit.

> Verse five, And there are varieties of ministries, and the same Lord.
>
> Verse six, And there are varieties of effects, but the same God who works all things in all persons.
>
> Verse seven, But to each one is given the manifestation of the spirit for the common good.
>
> Verse eight, for to one is given the word of wisdom through the spirit, and to another the word of knowledge according to the same spirit;
>
> Verse nine, to another faith by the same spirit, and to another gifts of healing by the one spirit,
>
> Verse 10, and to another the affecting of miracles, and to another prophecy, and to another the distinguishing of spirits, to another various kinds of tongues, and to another the interpretation of tongues.
>
> Verse 11, But one and the same spirit works all these things, distributing to each one individually just as he wills.

When we received the baptism in the Holy Spirit there is a variety of gifts that come to operate in our lives, and as we have already read, there are 3 gifts that reveal something, there are 3 gifts that say something, and there are 3 gifts that do something, it's also important to understand that not all nine gifts are operating at the same time in anyone's life.

In my own personal life, the gift of faith, the gift of praying for the sick, (Healing), the gift of distinguishing of spirits, (discerning) of spirits, speaking in (other tongues), as the spirit gives the utterance, and the gift to preach the gospel, which is (prophecy), no I am not a prophet, but I do have the gift of prophecy which is to preach, first Corinthians 14:3.

For you see God the Holy Spirit is not dead, but he is alive and well, and we do not run after gifts, but after a Christ likeness, to be transformed in the image of Jesus Christ.

In Galatians chapter 5: 22 But the fruit of the Spirit is love, joy, peace, patience, kindness, goodness, faithfulness,

Verse 23, gentleness, self-control; against such things there is no law.

Everything we will ever need to be successful children, men, providers, leaders, husbands, and assume any of the fivefold ministry gifts, is found in the baptism of the Holy Spirit, for without these gifts and fruits, we are not an example to a hurting and dying world, but our God reigns, and that his holy spirit can baptize the average Christian and give him those gifts.

The gifts of the Holy Spirit, and the fruit of the Holy Spirit, is a God given, distributed by the Holy Spirit as he wills, all of these variety of effects, it is done by God himself through the power of the Holy Spirit, working in us and through us.

But you may ask, is the baptism of the Holy Spirit for me today?

IS THE BAPTISM OF THE HOLY SPIRIT FOR ME TODAY?

Very good question, let's look at the Scriptures as you and will see what God says.

> **In the book of Acts chapter 1:8 But you shall receive power when the Holy Spirit has come upon you; and you shall be my witnesses both in Jerusalem, and in all Judea and Samaria, and even to the remotest part of the earth."**
>
> **In the book of Acts chapter 2:2,4 And suddenly there came from heaven and noise like a violent, rushing wind, and it filled the whole house where they were sitting.**
>
> **Verse three, And there appeared to them tongues as of fire distributing themselves, and they rested on each one of them.**
>
> **Verse four, And they were all filled with the Holy Spirit and began to speak with other tongues, as the spirit was giving them utterance.**
>
> **In the book of acts chapter 2:38,39 verse 38, And Peter said to them, "Repent, and let each of you be baptized in the name of Jesus Christ for the forgiveness of your sins; and you shall receive the gift of the Holy Spirit.**

Verse 39, "For the promise is for you and your children, and for all who are far off, as many as the Lord our God shall call to himself."

I hope the answer to this question has been answered, in order to fulfill the commission we have got to have supernatural power living within us, that power that they received in verse eight, is the Greek word dunamis, of that which manifests God's power, an explosive God given ability to share, and without it we cannot share the word of God.

And it is that same Holy Spirit who gives the utterance to speak in other tongues, and is that same Holy Spirit who gives us the gifts of the Holy Spirit, and it is that same Holy Spirit, who gives us the fruit of the Holy Spirit, and it is given to those who repent, and believes in Jesus Christ and are baptized, and then comes the promise.

For this particular promise found in verse 39 is for everyone in the Bible times, and anybody who believes in the Lordship of Jesus Christ and is baptized, for only the ones who are called by God to himself.

If you are not saved, bow your head right now and say with me dear heavenly father, I come to you in Jesus name, I repent of my sin, I turn my back on my old way of living, and I receive Jesus Christ into my life right now, come into my heart Lord Jesus, and be my Savior, and Lord, and baptized me in the precious Holy Spirit, with the gifts, and the fruit of the holy spirit in Jesus name, amen.

The gift of the Holy Spirit according to verse 39, is for us many as God himself called to himself, and you just said the sinner's prayer, and Jesus Christ of Nazareth just came into your heart, and according to second Corinthians chapter 5:17 you are a new creature in Christ Jesus, and on verse 38 it says that you shall receive the gift of the Holy Spirit, it's a guaranteed promise, to those who repent and are baptized in the name of the Lord Jesus, for the forgiveness of sins, and then we will receive the gift of the Holy Spirit, aren't you happy that God cannot lie, and that his holy word is forever settled in heaven.

I hope that so far what we have been reading about God the Holy Spirit, has stirred up your heart, and your desire to have holier walk with God, and seek him through prayer, through the reading of his holy word, through fasting, and through meditating on everything you have already read, because God does not lie.

Our heavenly father loves us and we are special people, we are God's greatest creation, and he wants to empower us, and live through us, thereby touching, loving, and reaching, hurting humanity as a whole.

Our God is an awesome God, who paid the ultimate price, to redeem fallen human beings, to live in them and through them by the power of the Holy Spirit, hallelujah, praise his holy name, amen, and amen.

GOD'S PLAN FOR MAN

God has six major reasons why he came in the person of Jesus Christ, now he has many more reasons, but he told me to write six of the most important ones, and the first one was to get us to repent, to turn our backs on sin and receive the free gift of eternal life, second, he came to save us, deliver us, to set us free, from the grips of hell, the third, was to give us the baptism in water, as an external manifestation of the inward faith, fourth, he came to make us whole, set us free from sickness disease and infirmities, Fifth, he came to give us the baptism in the Holy Spirit, so that we would have supernatural power against the enemy, and this way the gifts of the spirit and the fruit of the spirit would operate in our lives, and the sixth, he came to take us home, to provide the way, two wash us and cleanse us with his precious blood.

These are the most important six reasons why he came in the person of Jesus Christ.

Number one, (Repentance)

> **in the gospel of Matthew's chapter 3:1,2 Now in those days John the Baptist came, preaching in the wilderness of Judea, saying,**
>
> **Verse two, "Repent, for the kingdom of heaven is at hand."**

John the Baptist was the forerunner of Jesus Christ of Nazareth, and his message was about repentance, because the kingdom of heaven was at hand. We must all repent before we are saved from our guilt and shame, and be pardon from all our sin.

In the gospel of Matthew's chapter 3:11 "As for me, I baptize you with water for repentance, but he who is coming after me is mightier than I, and I am not fit to remove his sandals; he will baptize you with the Holy Spirit and fire.

Here we see how John the Baptist the forerunner of Jesus is preparing human beings, and how he is baptizing them in water for the repentance of their sins, but the one coming after him which was Jesus Christ, he was going to baptize them in the Holy Spirit and in fire.

In the gospel of Luke chapter 24:45, 47 Then he opened their minds to understand the Scriptures,

Verse 46, and he said to them, "As it is written, that the Christ should suffer and rise again from the dead the third day;

Verse 47, and that repentance for forgiveness of sins should be proclaimed in his name to all the nations, beginning from Jerusalem.

The first thing we need, is to have our minds open up to the gospel of Jesus Christ, so that we might understand the scriptures, that Jesus came to die and suffer for us, he was buried in a tomb, and on the third day rose again from the dead, as the sacrificed Lamb to take away the sins of the world, that includes you and me, and that people all over the world would repent, and receive him as Savior and Lord for the forgiveness of sins, and that they should start preaching this message of repentance in Jerusalem and to all the nations of the world.

Now when we go to Acts of the Apostles chapter 2:38 And Peter said to them, "Repent, and let each of you be baptized in the name of Jesus Christ for the forgiveness of your sins; and you shall receive the gift of Holy Spirit.

Here we see Peter in the book of the Acts of the Apostles preaching his message about repentance, and then he said be baptized in the name of the Lord Jesus Christ, for the forgiveness of your sins, and then you shall receive the gift of the Holy Spirit.
This is why a lot of people have tried to receive the baptism in Holy Spirit, and have not,
Because they have not repented, what is repentance?
Repentance, the Greek word for it is Metanoeo, which means a U-turn, a turnaround in thinking, hence signifies to change one's mind or purpose, a change for the better.
In other words a U-turn from our old thinking patterns, a U-turn and a turnaround from my old behavioral patterns, like a U-turn in the middle of the street with a car, to start heading in a different direction with Godly biblical principles.
Then acknowledge that we need to be saved, receive into our hearts the Lord Jesus Christ, Then go to a church get baptized in water, and only then are we ready for the baptism in the Holy Spirit, repentance, receive, be baptized, then receive the baptism in the Holy Spirit, there is a lot of people playing church, a lot of people being very religious, a lot of people mixing the world's philosophy, with Christianity, and they are not born again.

In the Acts of the Apostles chapter 17:30 "Therefore having overlooked the times of ignorance, God is now declaring to men that all everywhere should repent.

As you very well may see repentance is not an option is a command directly from God, for it is the only way we can have common union and fellowship with our heavenly father.

In the epistle to the Romans chapter 10:9, 10, v13 That if you confess with your mouth Jesus as Lord, and believe in your heart that God raised him from the dead, you shall be saved;

Verse 10, for with the heart man believes, resulting in righteousness, and with the mouth he confesses, resulting in salvation.

Verse 13, for "Whoever will call upon the name of the Lord will be saved."

Notice what it says here very clearly that we must confess with our mouth, that Jesus Christ is Lord, and believe in our hearts that God raised him from the dead, and if we need any proof of it we can fly over to Jerusalem to see an empty tomb, we shall be saved.

Please notice the underlined words; these are the prerequisites in order to be saved.

Number two, (salvation)

In the gospel of Matthew's chapter 1:21 "And she will bear a son; and you shall call his name Jesus, for it is he who will save his people from their sins."

In the gospel of Luke chapter 19:10 "For the Son of Man has come to seek and to save that which is lost."

Can you see in these two verses how clearly it is stated of our need to be saved, the word Jesus means Savior, the word Christ means anointed, Jesus Christ, the anointed Savior, it is very clear that Jesus Christ came to seek and to save those human beings that were lost.

> **In the gospel of Matthew's chapter 26:28 for this is my blood of the covenant, which is poured out for many for forgiveness of sins.**
>
> **In the gospel of John chapter 3:14, 17 "And as Moses lifted up the serpent in the wilderness, even so must the Son of Man be lifted up;**
>
> **Verse 15, that whoever believes may in him have eternal life.**
>
> **Verse 16, "For God so loved the world that he gave his only begotten son, that whoever believes in him should not perish, but have eternal life.**
>
> **Verse 17, "For God did not send the son into the world to judge the world, but that the world should be saved through him.**

The salvation of human beings can only be obtained through the new covenant, with the shed blood of Jesus Christ for the forgiveness of sins, and no other way.

When we acknowledge the Lordship of Jesus Christ and we repent of our sins, and we invite him into our hearts, his precious blood cleanses us from all sin, our spirit is regenerate, Got seals us with the Holy Spirit of promise, and we become a new born again Christian, and eternal life is deposited within us, the God kind of life.

God did not send Jesus into the world to condemn the world, but that the world would be saved through him, salvation is God's eternal goal, salvation for every human being on this planet.

In the epistle from Paul to the Romans chapter 5:8, 11 But God demonstrates his own love toward us, in that while we were yet sinners, Christ died for us.

Verse nine, Much more then, having now been justified by his blood, we shall be saved from the wrath of God through him.

Verse 10, For if while we were enemies, we were reconciled to God through the death of his son, much more, having been reconciled, we shall be saved by his life.

It is important to understand that the plan of God for redemption through the shed blood of Jesus Christ on the cross, happened almost 2013 years ago, and when we get the word of God in our hands and we read it, we are accepting his precious blood to cleanse us, his substitution AL sacrifice for us, and the salvation of our soul which happened back then.

God's eternal love is demonstrated towards us that Jesus Christ paid the penalty for us.

And with the shedding of his blood on the cross he justifies human beings in the sight of God, now it is not until people understand this that they are saved.

Jesus Christ's shed blood on the cross justified humanity in the sight of God, but that benefit cannot and will not work for us, until we repent and receive the free gift of eternal life, which is Jesus Christ, and then that justifiable shed blood on the cross becomes applicable in our lives, to cleanse us and make us just in the sight of God.

Even while we were yet sinners that justifiable shed blood was done in our stead, God did not wait for us to be righteous for him to justify us, that method of saving humanity was instituted by God Almighty through the sacrificed Lamb on the cross.

Now when we receive Jesus Christ into our hearts, that total redemptive work on the cross, cleanses us and makes us righteous in God's eyes, how much more now having been reconciled, we shall be saved through his life.

The plan of God for the salvation of human beings becomes applicable in our lives after we repent and receive the sacrificed Lamb into our hearts, and it happens through the Holy Spirit's seal in our hearts, Ephesians 4:13.

In the epistle of Paul to the Romans chapter 3:23 for all have sinned and fall short of the glory of God.

The epistle of Paul to the Romans chapter 6:23 For the wages of sin is death, but the free gift of God is eternal life in Christ Jesus our Lord.

So according to God's plan, which is the salvation of human beings, what we see on verse 23 is that all human beings have sinned and come short of God's glory, without exception, someone said to me recently They did not need to be saved because they were good people, and they did right by other people, and they'd never hurt anybody, so why would they need to be saved?

Because God said it, we all have sinned, if God said it, we must believe it and that settles it.

And that's not all, for the wages of sin is death, but the free gift of God is eternal life in Jesus Christ.

All human beings that are not saved, are in spiritual death in relationship to a holy and spiritual God, and also our bodies are already dying, and ultimately will die and be buried, this is why we need to be regenerate in our spirit by the Holy Spirit, that we may have a relationship with a living God who is a spirit, and later be given a glorified body to live for eternity.

Number three, (Water baptism)

> in the gospel of Matthew's chapter 3:16,17 And after being baptized, Jesus went up immediately from the water, and behold, the heavens were opened, and he saw the Spirit of God descending as a dove, and coming upon him,
>
> Verse 17, behold, a voice out of the heavens, saying, "This is my beloved son, in whom I am well pleased."

Water baptism is a must and is also instituted by God himself, when even our Lord and Savior had to be baptized by John the Baptist, and notice also how he came up out of the water, which means he was submerged in the water.

Water baptism should not be sprinkled, the person should wait until they're old enough to believe in the Lordship of Jesus Christ, and only then be submerged in water, just like Jesus.

In the Jewish tradition when people were born, on their eighth day, they were presented to the high priest in the synagogue, so they would be circumcised, and be offered up to serve God, and be dedicated to God, they were not baptized in water as an infant.

Like some traditional religions that when the child is born, they are taken to the priest to be sprinkled water upon their heads, and supposedly there by baptizing them, that is an error according to biblical principles.

When Jesus was born, on the eights day he was taken to the synagogue where he was circumcised, and offered up to God in prayer as the Jewish custom was.

So water baptism has to be submerged, and only to the believer in Jesus Christ.

In the gospel of Mark chapter 16:16 "He who has believed and has been baptized shall be saved; but he who has disbelieved shall be condemned.

In the Acts of the Apostles chapter 2:38 And Peter said to them, "Repent, and let each of you be baptized in the name of Jesus Christ for the forgiveness of your sins; and you shall receive the gift of the Holy Spirit.

It is important to say something here, when the thief at the right hand of Jesus on the cross said to him, remember me when you come into your kingdom, Jesus said right away today you will be with me in paradise, this man didn't even repent, this man wasn't even baptized in water, but he said to Jesus remember me, he acknowledged that Jesus was the King of Kings and the Lord of lords, so in order to go to heaven you don't necessarily have to be baptized in water.

Water baptism is an outward testimony that you have been buried to your old nature, and that you have been resurrected out of the water into a new life, it is an outward testimony of an inward conviction, and it is what you do after you have been saved.

In the Acts of the apostles chapter 10:47, 48 "Surely no one can refuse the water for these to be baptized who have received the Holy Spirit just as we did, can he?"

Verse 48, And he ordered them to be baptized in the name of Jesus Christ.

Then they asked him to stay on for a few days.

In these passages we see that they were believers and that they had received the baptism in the Holy Spirit, and then they were baptized, so the order is first to repent, second to believe, and then normally to be baptized, and then you receive the baptism in the Holy Spirit, but as you can see in this particular scenario they believed, then they received the baptism in the Holy Spirit, and then they were baptized, so the order of events may be totally different with different people in different scenarios.

In the acts of the apostles chapter 19:3,5 And he said, "Into what then were you baptized?" And they said, "Into John's baptism," the gospel of Matthew chapter 28:19,20 "Go therefore and make disciples of all nations, baptizing them in the name of the father and of the son and of the Holy Spirit,

Verse 20, teaching them to observe all that I commanded you; and low, I am with you always, even to the end of the age,"

John the forerunner of Jesus baptized people on to repentance, but when we received Jesus Christ as Savior and Lord, we should then be baptized in water, and then we should go throughout the whole world making disciples of all nations, and baptizing them in the name of the father the son and of the Holy Spirit.

And his promise is that he will be with us always even to the end of the age.

If you were baptized when you were just a child in your tradition, then my suggestion is to get baptized again the rite way, by submersion, after you surrender your will to Christ's in obedience to his word, they should also give you a certificate to the fact.

Number four, (divine healing)

In the gospel of Matthew's chapter 8:16, 17 And when evening had come, they brought to him many who were demon-possessed; and he cast out the spirits with a word, and healed all who were ill,

Verse 17, in order that what was spoken through Isaiah the prophet might be fulfilled, saying, "He himself took our infirmities, and carried away our diseases,"

God's divine purpose for you and me is that we would be completely whole, sickness disease and infirmity has no right upon our lives, because Jesus took all infirmities with him, and he carried away all the enemies' diseases. Notice the word demon possessed, and he cast out the spirits with a word, and healed all who were ill.

Christians cannot be demon possessed, Christians can be, influenced, Christians can be (oppressed, Christians can be tormented, especially if we're disobeying the word of God, the Bible says that a spirit of disobedience, or a spirit of rebellion is influencing our lives, thereby causing us to be moved by the flesh and not the Holy Spirit.

The born-again spirit filled Christian needs to know how to pray, bind the enemy in Jesus name, and command it to leave the person's life, that we are praying for, Jesus Christ defeated all principalities, and powers, and rulers, and spiritual wickedness in high places, and Jesus Christ of Nazareth lives within us, that is why he delegated that authority in his name, Luke's gospel 10; 19. We'll talk more about that God-given authority later on.

In the gospel of Luke chapter 7:21, 22 At that very time he cured many people of diseases and afflictions and evil spirits; and he granted sight to many who were blind.

Verse 22, And he answered and said to them, "Go and report to John what you have seen and heard: the blind receive sight, the lame walk, the lepers are cleansed, and the deaf hear, the dead are raised up, the poor have the gospel preached to them.

This is the will of God for our lives that we would be cured from all diseases and afflictions, and that evil spirits will not influence, oppress, and torment our lives anymore.

Every Christian has received spiritual sight, every Christian has a new walk, every Christian has been cleansed, every Christian has a spiritual ear, every Christian's lives have been raised up from the dead, and every Christian is no longer poor because the Gospel has been preached to us, and that is the gospel, the unmerited good news.

Divined Healing, divine deliverance, and divine health are our inheritance in Jesus name.

In the gospel of Luke chapter 10:9 and heal those in it who are sick, and say to them, the kingdom of God has come near to you,'

Here we see how the Lord Jesus Christ assembled 70 disciples, and send them two and two ahead of him to every city and place where he himself was going, and he said as you go into those cities, and into those homes, heal the sick, and tell them that the kingdom of God has come. The kingdom of God did come, and is raining within us, and we are all disciples of Jesus Christ, and are commanded by himself to go and lay hands on the sick and in the name of Jesus Christ bind, rebuke, those evil spirits and cast them out, just as those disciples of old did.

> **In the epistle of first Peter chapter 2:24 and he himself bore our sins in his body on the cross, that we might die to sin and live to righteousness; for by his wounds you were healed**

That we might die to sin, and live to righteousness, for by his stripes, wounds, you were healed. Please notice the past tense, not that were going to get healed, but that we were healed, then when you act upon what happened for you and me 2013 years ago, and you realize that sickness disease and infirmity has no legal right up on your body, you can actually lay hands on your own self and pray that oppression to get off of you, or cursed it to die off of you, in Jesus name, amen.

Number five, (baptism in the Holy Spirit)

> **in the gospel of Matthew's chapter 3:11 "As for me, I baptize you with water for repentance, but he who is coming after me is mightier than I, and I am not fit to remove his sandals; He will baptize you with the Holy Spirit and fire.**

In many denominations that do not believe in the baptism of the Holy Spirit, as a second manifestation of grace, they believe that when you got saved, that you were sealed with the Holy Spirit of promise in Ephesians 4:30 and 1:13 and that is true, but then comes the baptism, or the in filling, as you develop your communion with God.

When I was saved a tremendous vacuum lifted from my heart, Jesus came to take up residence within me, and I knew that I knew that I was saved, but two to three weeks later I had a dream and the Lord revealed to me that sister fields would lay hands on my head in order to receive the baptism in the Holy Spirit, and sure enough I went to her and said sister fields please pray for me, and she did, and at that time nothing truly happened. O but that night I was sleeping about three in the morning, and suddenly I awoke up and I sense a tingling sensation from the crown of my head to the soles of my feet, and a supernatural warmth came into my heart, and ever since I have had a hunger, a desire, and a motivation to become knowledgeable with God's holy word, a share it with everybody I come into contact.

The baptism in the Holy Spirit is the spirit of the living God, bringing into our hearts the gifts of the Holy Spirit, and the fruits of the Holy Spirit which we already talked about.

> **In the gospel of John chapter 7:37, 39 Now on the last day, the great day of the feast, Jesus stood and cried out, saying, "If any man is thirsty, let him come to me and drink.**

> **Verse 38, "He who believes in me, as the Scriptures said, 'From his innermost being shall flow rivers of living water,'**

> **Verse 39, But this he spoke of the spirit, whom those who believed in him were to receive; for the Spirit was not yet given, because Jesus was not yet glorified.**

Here in the gospel of John we see it prophesied already that Jesus was going to go way in order to send forth the helper, the comforter, the precious Holy Spirit, whom every believer would receive, and the moment he was glorified and went to the right hand of the father, he sends forth what we are about to read in acts chapter 2:1, 4.

> **In the Acts of the Apostles chapter 2:1, 4 And when the day of Pentecost had come, they were all together in one place.**

Verse two, and suddenly there came from heaven a noise like a violent, rushing wind, and it filled the whole house where they were sitting.

Verse three, And there appeared to them tongues as of fire distributing themselves, and they rested on each one of them.

Verse four, and they were all filled with the Holy Spirit and began to speak with other tongues, as the spirit was giving them utterance.

In this particular event the spirit was then given to those who believed on the Lord Jesus Christ, that prophecy of the gospel of John 7:39 was finally manifested not long after Jesus was taken up into heaven as he had promised.

In the Acts of the Apostles chapter 10:44 While Peter was still speaking these words, the Holy Spirit fell upon all of those who were listening to the message.

In this event we see Peter baptized in the Holy Spirit preaching the gospel to them, and as he was doing it, the spirit came upon the believers who were listening to the gospel.

In the Acts of the Apostles chapter 19:6 And when Paul had laid his hands upon them, Holy Spirit came on them, and they began speaking with tongues and prophesied.

In the epistle of Paul to the Romans chapter 14:17 for the kingdom of God is not eating and drinking, but righteousness and peace and joy in the Holy Spirit.

In first Corinthians chapter 12:13 For by one spirit we were all baptized into one body, whether Jews or Greeks, whether slaves or free, and we were all made to drink of one spirit.

So as you have read for yourself in all of these paragraphs the spirit of the living God is God, and that he wants to baptize us with his Holy Spirit, or give us an infilling of the Holy Spirit, or give us the Holy Spirit with his manifested power, however we want to put it, it is a second manifestation of grace, and an experience to be had.

Number six, (the second coming of Jesus Christ)

in the gospel of Matthew's chapter 24:27 "For just as the lightning comes from the east, and flashes even to the west, so shall the coming of the Son of Man be.

Every person that has become a believer in Jesus Christ our Lord is waiting for a glorious time, when he and the church will be resurrected, rapture, taken away, snatched away, in the twinkling of an eye and we will ever be with the Lord in heaven.

In first Thessalonians chapter 4:16, 17 For the Lord himself will descend from heaven with a shout, with the voice of the Archangel, and with the trumpet of God; and the dead in Christ shall rise first.

Verse 17, That we who are alive and remain shall be caught up together with them in the clouds to meet the Lord in the air, and thus we shall always be with the Lord.

As the song says soon and very soon we will see the King, can you believe what a glorious day awaits us to see the Lord descend from heaven with a shout, with the voice of an Archangel, and with the trumpet of God, can you believe what the trumpet will sound like, I don't know about you reading this book but I'm excited just reading up on it.

Now of course the dead in Christ will rise first, but we who are alive will be caught up with them in the air, and thus we shall be with the Lord forever, hallelujah. That is going to be a glorious second coming that every true born-again Holy Spirit filled believer is waiting for.

In Hebrews chapter 9:28 so Christ also, having been offered once to bear the sins of many, shall appear a second time for salvation without reference to sin, to those who eagerly await him.

When he comes the second time he will have absolutely nothing to do with sin, his second coming is only to take us away, for on this second coming, he will not step foot on earth.

In second Peter chapter 3:10 But the day of the Lord will come like a thief, in which the heavens will pass away with a roar and the elements will be destroyed with intense heat, and the earth and its works will be burned up.

In revelations chapter 1:7 Behold, He is coming with the clouds, and every eye will see him, even those who pierced him; and all the tribes of the earth will mourn over him. Even so. Amen.

Every eye will see him, and all the tribes will mourn over him, and even so Lord Jesus come.

And in revelations chapter 22:12 "Behold, I am coming quickly, and my reward is with me, to render to every man according to what he has done.

So my brother and my sister those of you reading this wonderful book, our precious Lord Jesus is coming soon, and we must be ready, cleansed and washed in his precious blood.

WHO AM I, MY IDENTITY, WRITES AND PRIVILEGES, AND GOD GIVEN POWER

As we look into these very important but controversial topics, we will explore God's view, God's word, God's thoughts, and ultimately who we are by receiving Jesus Christ as Savior and Lord.

We will start by excluding the views and ways of people that are negative, derogatory, demeaning, dogmatic, judgmental, and critical views, from a father who was not very loving, from a mother who was not very happy, from brothers and sisters who were judgmental and jealous of us, from our friends and coworkers who don't like us very much, from every teacher that we have had in our childhood, including some pastors and biblical teachers, and even brothers and sisters in Christ from our local church, from every girlfriend, boyfriend, husband, wife, or even children that for some reason do not like us, do not approve of us, do not appreciate our talents and abilities, and do not take serious the calling of God on our lives.

Thank God,(I am), what God says, (I am)

In the epistle of Paul to the Romans chapter 12:3 For I say, through the grace given unto me, to every man that is among you, not to think of himself more highly than he ought to think; but to think soberly, according as God has dealt to every man the measure of faith.

Our thought life about ourselves, about our self-worth, about our self-value, has got to come only from the word of Almighty God, and not the opinions of anybody else, here we see the apostle Paul writing to the church in Rome, and telling them, for I say, through the grace given unto me, he acknowledged that grace was given unto him, so as he writes he is saying to them to every man that is among you, not to think of himself more highly than he ought to think, when you develop a thought life, when you develop a self-worth, develop a self-value, that is higher than the word of God, or that it contradicts the word of God, or it has arrogance and pride in it, that is when you are proud full and boastful about yourself, and you are not thinking according to Scriptures. And this is why I wrote this book.

But to think soberly, according as God has dealt to every man the measure of faith.

When the sinner repents, and he acknowledges the need of a Savior, and he invites that Savior to come into his life, and forgive all his sins, Jesus Christ comes into the human soul by the power of the Holy Spirit, and he causes the human spirit to come alive in relationship to God.

GOD SAYS, THAT I AM
(A NEW CREATURE IN CHRIST JESUS)

In second Corinthians chapter 5:17 Therefore if any man be in Christ, he is a new creature: old things are passed away; behold all things are become new.

When Jesus Christ comes into your life he brings a measure of faith in you, and from that moment on you would be thinking soberly if you say to everybody that you are a brand-new creation, a new creature, a new person, a born-again believer, with no past. You would not be lying, but you would be saying exactly what God said, his opinion.

The Bible says that we are a new creature in Christ, how should we feel when we read these passages, and like Nicodemus being old, we are being told that we are a new creation, that all things have passed away and behold all things are become new.

GOD SAYS, THAT I AM
(BORN OF AN INCORRUPTIBLE SEED)

In first Peter chapter 1:23 Being born again, not of corruptible seed, but of incorruptible, by the word of God, which liveth and abideth forever.

The born again believer has a supernatural rebirth with a seed that lives and abides forever, which is the word of God as we read earlier in the beginning of this book, the born again believer experiences 2 birth's, one the natural birth from a mom and dad, and the second from an eternal supernatural seed planted within the human being, it is called a spiritual rebirth. Or born again.

In first John chapter 3:9 whosoever is born of God doth not commit sin; for his seed remaineth in him: and he cannot sin, because he is born of God.

A person born of the seed of God does not practice sin, because the conviction of the Holy Spirit rebukes him, and if he decides to practice sin, his life will be totally miserable, but every born-again Christian sins, because he is imperfect, because he is immature, because he is undeveloped, because he needs to grow up spiritually, and it is he who the enemy targets his fiery darts to the most, this way he would blame Christians and God.

GOD SAYS, THAT I AM
(BORN AGAIN SPIRITUALLY)

Jesus Christ explained it better in the gospel of John chapter 3:3,10 Jesus answered and said unto him, Verily, verily, I say unto thee, Accept a man be born again, he cannot see the kingdom of God.

Verse four, Nicodemus saith unto him, how can a man be born when he is old? Can he enter the second time into his mother's womb, and be born?

Verse five, Jesus answered, Verily, verily, I say unto thee, except a man be born of water and of the spirit, he cannot enter into the kingdom of God.

Verse six, That which is born of the flesh is flesh; and that which is born of the spirit is spirit.

Verse seven, Marvel not that I said unto thee, ye must be born again.

Jesus Christ explained to Nicodemus who happen to be a very important person in the Sanhedrin, a very important religious ruler, that his traditional religiosity was not enough to see or enter the kingdom of God, but that he needed to be born again, have a spiritual rebirth, have a born again new life, when you look at it from a natural standpoint it makes no sense.

He was a good man who studied the word of God, he was a religious ruler of his age, he knew the Torah very well, he was very well versed in Moses law, and he was equal to a cardinal from our religious tradition universal upbringing.

But Jesus Christ said to Nicodemus Marvel not that I say to you,(you must be born again), and obviously him being between 45 and 68 years old asked him, how can this be, how can I enter my mother's womb a second time and be born again?

Verse eight, The wind bloweth were it listeth, and thou hearest the sound thereof, but canst not tell whence it cometh, and whither it goeth: so is everyone that is born of the spirit.

Verse nine, Nicodemus answered and said unto him, how can these things be?

Verse 10, Jesus answered and said unto him, Art thou a master of Israel, and knowest not these things?

Jesus Christ said that we do not have an option, and that in order to see or enter into the kingdom of God, we had to be born again, to have a spiritual rebirth, and be a born again Christian.

GOD SAYS, THAT I AM
(A SPIRITUAL BABE IN CHRIST)

In first Corinthians chapter 3:1, 2,3 And I, brethren, could not speak unto you as unto spiritual, but as unto carnal, even as unto babes in Christ.

Verse two, I have fed you with milk, and not with meat: for hitherto ye were not able to bear it, neither yet now are ye able.

Verse three, For you are yet carnal: for whereas there is among you envying, and strife, and divisions, are ye not carnal, and walk as men?

Notice here the apostle Paul could not speak to them as fully grown spiritual man, but as babes in Christ, and he said he had fed them milk, not strong meat, because they were not able to bear the teachings, and the reason why they cannot bear it, it was because they were carnal, and on verse three he goes on to explain how he knew they were carnal. This is why we all need to grow up, mature, and be transformed by the renewing of our minds, more on this topic later on in what we should do in Christ.

GOD SAYS, THAT I AM (A CHILD OF GOD)

In the gospel of John chapter 1:11, 13 He came onto his own, and his own received him not.

Verse 12, But as many as received him, to them gave he power to become the sons of God, even to them that believe on his name:

Verse 13, which were born, not of blood, nor of the will of the flesh, nor of the will of man, but of God.

I am not only born of the will of man, but I am born of the will of God, it was God's idea to redeem us, it was God's idea to make as his child, it was God's idea to give us the spiritual new birth. By receiving Jesus Christ into our hearts, our spirit is awakened, regenerate, comes alive, and it is restored just like Adam and Eve in the garden, and we become a spirit being, possessing a soul and living inside our body, and we experienced the rebirth by the will of God.

In the first epistle of John 4:7 Beloved, let us love one another: for love is of God; and everyone that loveth is born of God, and knoweth God.

In the first epistle of John 5:1 Whosoever believeth that Jesus is the Christ is born of God: and everyone that loveth him that begat loveth him also that is begotten of him.

God is commanding us to love one another, because the agape kind of love has been poured into our hearts, the God kind of life has come into our lives, and our spirit is saturated with that supernatural nature of God, thank God we are now able to love, and this is where all the disciples around the world will see that we are truly born again, when we have love one for another, this is the only way we can demonstrate to the world that we are born of God.

GOD SAYS, THAT I AM
(AN OVERCOMER IN CHRIST)

In the first epistle of John 5:4 For whosoever is born of God overcomes the world: and this is the victory that overcomes the world, even our faith.

This is the promise for anybody reading this book or anybody in the world; it says that whosoever is born of God overcomes the world. Let's look at what the Bible calls the world.

In the first epistle of John 2:16 For all that is in the world, the lust of the flesh, the lust of the eyes, and the pride of life, is not of the father, but as of the world.

God says that through faith in Jesus Christ, we can overcome everything that is in this world, which includes the lust of our flesh, or the temptation that comes against our flesh, seducing every member of our being and bringing us into captivity becoming a slave once again.

God says that through faith in Jesus Christ, we can overcome everything that is in this world, which includes the lust of our eyes, or the temptation that seduces our eyes through lust, through the obsession of obtaining material things, through the temptation of seeing others prosper more than us, and other temptations that we see daily with our eyes.

God says that through faith in Jesus Christ, we could overcome everything that is in this world, which includes the pride of life, through greed, through looks, through material possessions, through better careers, through glamour, and Hollywood's glory.

God says that whoever is born of him overcomes the world, which includes the lust of the flesh, the lust of the eyes, and the pride of life, God says that I am an overcomer, and if God said it in his holy word, and we have already read it, then I am what God says I am, and that settles it.

In the first epistle of John 3:1, 2 Behold, what manner of love the father has bestowed upon us, that we should be called the sons of God: therefore the world knoweth us not, because it knew him not.

Verse two, Beloved, now are we the sons of God, and it doth not yet appear what we shall be: but we know that, when he shall appear, we shall be like him; for we shall see him as he is.

What manner of love the father has bestowed upon us, by sending Jesus Christ to live within our hearts, so that we would be called the regenerate sons of God, and on verse two it says beloved, now are we the sons of God, born of God, by the seed of God, by the spiritual rebirth of God, by being a new created creature, with a heavenly father.

Now when we see him face-to-face we shall be like him, for we shall see him as he is, we would have already received a glorified body, and be completely redeemed in spirit soul and body, right now we are spiritually born again, not physically, but when we are raptured we will receive a glorified body to live for eternity.

In the epistle of Paul to the Romans chapter 8:15, 16 For ye have not received the spirit of bondage again to fear; but ye have received the spirit of adoption, whereby we cry, Abba father.

Verse 16, The spirit itself beareth witness with our spirit, that we are the children of God.

Once again we see it all, no born again spirit filled believer has received a spirit of bondage to fear all over again; but we have received a spirit of adoption, whereby we can cry, Abba father, Abba father, God is our heavenly father and we are his children, and he is very well concerned about our well-being spiritually, mentally, physically, relationally, financially.

As a caring loving, compassionate, and merciful heavenly father, he cares for every area of our lives, he is good, he is merciful, he is gentle, he is tender, and he loves us with an everlasting love, an agape love which is unconditional, and it never changes regardless of what we have done, don't you love him, aren't you grateful, appreciative to him, he is truly worthy of praise, adoration, and to be exalted for there is none like him, hallelujah, I love you Lord.

Our maker, our Redeemer, our deliverer, our new life giver, and our eternity guarantee.

I sense such a precious Holy Spirit in this entire room right now that I have to stop to worship him, and magnify him for he is good and worthy, that every knee will bow, and that every tong will confess that Jesus Christ is Lord to the glory of the father, hallelujah.

In this new dispensation of the unmerited favor which is the grace of God, aren't we glad that we can have an identity not based on other people's opinion, but according to God's opinion, on what he has made us in Christ Jesus, who we truly are, thanks to the shedding of his precious blood on the cross, in order to cleanse us, to deliver us, and to set us free from the opinion of others, and to liberate us from the bondage and the slavery of sin, and the grip that the kingdom of darkness had upon us, should we be static and jumping up and down, thank God, I am, what God says, I am, and he said it and that settles it.

GOD SAYS, THAT I AM (DELIVERED FROM THE KINGDOM OF DARKNESS)

In Colossians chapter 1:13 Who has delivered us from the power of darkness, and hath translated us into the kingdom of his dear son:

Verse 14, in whom we have redemption through his blood, even the forgiveness of sins.

We have been delivered from the kingdom of darkness, and we have been translated, or inserted into the kingdom of his dear son, now our eyes can see the kingdom of God, now we have entered the kingdom of God, through the regenerate, and born again spiritual experience, we are spiritually born again into a new kingdom, with a new King Jesus Christ.

In Christ we are redeemed with his precious blood, which he paid the ultimate price to bring us back for fellowship with him, before Jesus shed his blood we belong to the kingdom of darkness, and we were alienated from the commonwealth of Israel, and we were blinded, we were ensnared, and the judgment of heaven was upon us.

In Colossians chapter 2:14, 15 Blotting out the handwriting of ordinances that was against us, which was contrary to us, and he took it out of the way, nailing it to his cross;

Verse 15, And having spoiled principalities and powers, he made a show of them openly, triumphing over them in it.

When the Bible says blotting out the handwriting of ordinances that was against us, is talking about the judgment of God that was passed upon humanity on the garden of Eden, and because Adam and Eve committed high treason we were given over to a kingdom of darkness, blinded by the enemy, and the judgment of God was upon us, but the important part of it is that Jesus Christ of Nazareth took it out of the way, he nailed it on his cross, that ordinance passed upon humanity by God's judgment has been lifted, thanks to the blood of Jesus.

And not only did the blood of Jesus canceled that ordinance that was against us, but he went ahead and spoiled principalities and powers, and spiritual wickedness in high places, destroying the power that the kingdom of darkness had upon us, thereby delivering us and giving us Victory, Jesus was the conqueror, this is why the Bible says that we are more than conquerors through him that loved us, he conquered it for us and gave us the victory, Amen.

In the sacrifice carried out by Jesus Christ's on Calvary, he obtained many benefits for us, number one, to set human bring free from the judgment of heaven upon them, number two; he delivered us from the kingdom of darkness and translated us into the kingdom of his dear son. He broke the power and legal write that kingdom of darkness had over us, he paid the ransom for the purchase of his prized possession, and number three, he conquered all principalities and powers of the enemy's legal right upon us, aren't we jumping up and down yet.

GOD SAYS, THAT I AM (THE RIGHTEOUSNESS OF GOD IN CHRIST)

In the second epistle of Paul to the Corinthians 5:21 He made him who knew no sin to be sin in our behalf, that we might become the righteousness of God in him.

While Jesus was on the cross he said father why has thou forsaken me, in that fraction of a second the sin of all humanity was put upon him and God cannot look upon sin, he bore the sin of the world, in other words he who knew no sin became sin, you're sin, my sin, every human being's sin's, past, present, and every future sin you and I will commit has already been paid for, and put upon him, that is why God could not look upon him, he was our substitution, we should have been nailed to the cross, our sins demanded a penalty and a punishment, but he took our place instead, with a divined supernatural purpose, that you and I would become the righteousness of God in him.

Righteousness, = the Greek word (Dikaiosune) which is the character or quality of being right or just in the sight of God.

But for the most part he uses it of the gracious gift of God to men whereby all who believe on the Lord Jesus Christ are brought into right relationship with God.

His righteousness is unattainable by obedience to any law, or by any merits of man's own, or any other condition than that of faith in Christ.

The man who believes in Jesus Christ becomes 'The righteousness of God in him.

And in Christ he becomes all that God requires a man to be, all that he could never be in himself.

Righteousness has been imputed upon human beings just as Faith was.

And when Faith is acted upon it brings the soul into vital union with God in Christ.

In Romans chapter 6:1, 11 What shall we say then? Are we to continue in sin that grace might increase?

Verse two, May it never be! How shall we who died to sin still live in it?

Verse three, or do you not know that all of us who have been baptized into Christ Jesus have been baptized into his death?

Verse four, Therefore we have been buried with him through baptism into death, in order that as Christ was raised from the dead to the glory of the father, so we too might walk in newness of life

verse five, For if we have become united with him in the likeness of his death, certainly we shall also in the likeness of his resurrection,

Verse six, knowing this, that our old self was crucified with him, that our body of sin might be done away with, that we should no longer be slaves to sin;

Verse seven, for he who has died is freed from sin.

Verse eight, Now if we have died with Christ, we believe that we shall also live with him,

Verse nine, knowing that Christ, having been raised from the dead, never to die again; death no longer is a master over him.

Verse 10, For the death that he died, he died to sin, once for all; but the life that he lives, he leaves to God.

Verse 11, Even so consider yourselves to be dead to sin, but alive to God in Christ Jesus.

It took me almost 10 years to understand my positional death in Christ, and his attributed righteousness to my life, these two words have haunted me throughout all these years in my relationship with God through Christ, because the enemy kept Bringing to my mind, my unworthiness, my sin, my shortcomings, my imperfections, my faults, my immaturity, my bad relationships, and lots of other things that I did even while not knowing it, the enemy had me in a merry-go-round, with a poor old me syndrome, which I will never get anywhere thought life.

I never understood the positional righteousness imputed upon me, versus the righteous way I should treat other people, and learn to live a Just life, or the righteous way I should stand before our heavenly father in prayer, with the enemy constantly reminding me what a worthless piece of trash I was, and reminding me of all the mistakes that I had done, and even in a Pentecostal church I receive Jesus Christ into my heart 36 times, every time I would sin knowingly or unknowingly, I thought I would lose my salvation, until one day I got on my knees and God himself said to me how many times will my son have to die on the cross for you?

Then he took me first John chapter 1:8, 10 if we say that we have no sin, we are deceiving ourselves, and the truth is not in us.

Verse nine; if we confess our sins, he is faithful and righteous to forgive us our sins and to cleanse us from all unrighteousness.

Verse 10, if we say that we have not sinned, we make him a liar, and his word is not in us.

Then I understood the difference between position ally, and progressively.

Then I understood my positional righteousness from God attributed to me, in Christ.

Then I understood my positional death in Christ from Romans six that we just read.

Then I understood being right or just in the sight of God.

Then I understood the gracious gift of God given to men.

Then I understood that receiving Jesus Christ into my life, the measure of Faith was deposited with in me, and with it also came the righteousness of God. Romans12:3.

Then I understood that the free gift of righteousness could not be obtained by any obedience to any mosaic law, or by any of man's merits, or good deeds.

Then I understood that I had become all that God required of me, through the death, burial, and resurrection of the Lord Jesus Christ.

I am the father of two wonderful children, and the grandfather of four grandchildren, and when my two children were born in my family, they received my DNA, they received my blood, they received my love, they received my protection, they received my instruction, they received my correction, they received my discipline, they received my undivided attention, they received their rights and privileges, I helped them receive their identity, and some day they will receive the inheritance am going to leave them.

And from the time they were born as new creatures in my family, and they started to develop their organs, and started to walk, and started to speak, and started school, and became adolescent's, and became adults, and now happily married.

They made thousands of mistakes, they said a lot of wrong things, they behaved wrong a lot of times, they put their foot in their mouth many times, they would make wrong choices, they would find wrong relationships, they would date the wrong people, they went places and did things that were not in agreement with me, they disobeyed me many a times, they let me down many a times, they even argued with me contradicting my teachings, but as they were being developed, but as they were growing up, but as they were being matured, but as they were developing their relationship with me, they knew they could confess their faults and failures, and shortcomings, and confess to me everyone of their mistakes, and they knew that my love for them was eternal, and that I would forgive them instantly.

But at the end of the day, my DNA is still in them, my blood is still in them, my seed is still in them, my love has never grown cold for them, their rights and privileges in relationship to me have not changed, and I still love them will all of my heart.

There's a huge difference between who they are in relationship to me, versus the development of their relationship to me, relationship is one thing, while birthright is another.

Now getting back to Romans 6:2 how shall we who died to sin (position ally), still live in it, (progressively), on this one verse you see the duality of our relationship to God.

In Romans 6:4 therefore we have been buried with him through baptism into death, (position ally), in order that as Christ was raised from the dead to the glory of the father, so we too might walk in newness of life, (progressively).

In Romans 6:5 for if we have become united with him in the likeness of his death, (position ally) certainly we shall also in the likeness of his resurrection. (Progressively).

In Romans 6:6 knowing this, that our old self was crucified with him, (position ally) that our body of sin might be done away with, (position ally) that we should no longer be slaves to sin (progressively).

In Romans 6:7 four he who has died (position ally), is freed from sin (progressively).

In Romans 6:8 now if we have died with Christ, (position ally) we believe that we shall also live with him (progressively).

In Romans 6:9 knowing that Christ, having been raised from the dead, never to die again; death no longer is a master over him.

In Romans 6:10 for the death that he died, he died to sin, once for all; but the life that he lives, he lives to God.

In Romans 6:11 Even so consider yourselves to be dead to sin, (position ally) but alive to God in Christ Jesus (progressively).

So you see here the difference between (position ally), which is a gift, and (progressively) which is an act of our will.

So position ally we cannot sin, but progressively when we do sin, we can confess it to our heavenly father and he is faithful and just to forgive us and to cleanse us from all unrighteousness, progressively that is God's method for us to be right and righteous in his sight.

Now in John 1:8 if we say that we have no sin, we are deceiving ourselves, and the truth is not in us.

In John 1:9 if we confess our sins, he is faithful and righteous to forgive us our sins and to cleanse us from all unrighteousness.

In John 1:10 if we say that we have not sinned, we make him a liar, and his word is not in us.

Just as natural children, as they are developing their relationship with us, they make thousands of mistakes, and they have the assurance that we will forgive them instantly, so it is with our heavenly father, as we are developing our relationship with him, we make thousands of mistakes, because were immature, because we are imperfect, because we are in the development of our relationship with him, when we can confess our faults and failures he is faithful and just to forgive us and cleanse us.

The righteousness of God in Christ imputed upon us, attributed to us through faith in Jesus Christ (position ally) and the unrighteousness of sin forgiven and cleanse from us when we confess our sins (progressively).

So I can boldly say without fear of contradiction, that I am the righteousness of God in Christ (position ally) and that I will live a righteous life with other human beings, (progressively), hallelujah, praise his holy name.

GOD SAYS, THAT I AM,
(A MEMBER OF CHRIST'S BODY)

In the first epistle of Paul to the Corinthians chapter 12:12, 27,

> Verse 12, For as the body is one, and have many members, and all the members of that one body, being many, are one body: so also is Christ.
>
> Verse 13, For by one Spirit are we all baptized into one body, whether we be Jews or Gentiles, whether we be bond or free; and have been all made to drink into one Spirit.
>
> Verse 14, For the body is not one member, but many.
>
> Verse 15, If the foot shall say, because I am not a the hand, I am not of the body; is it therefore not of the body?
>
> Verse 16, And if the ear shall say, because I am not the eye, in my not of the body; is it therefore not of the body?
>
> Verse 17, If the whole body were an eye, where were the hearing? If the whole were hearing, where were the smelling?
>
> Verse 18, But now hath God set the members every one of them in the body, as it has pleased him.
>
> Verse 19, And if they were all one member, where were the body?

Verse 20, But now are they many members, yet but one body.

Verse 21, And the eye cannot say on to the hand, I have no need of thee: nor again the head to the feet, I have no need of you.

Verse 22, Nay, much more those members of the body, which seem to be more feeble, are necessary:

Verse 23, And those members of the body, which we think to be less honorable, upon these we bestow more abundant honor; and our uncomely parts have more abundant comeliness.

Verses 24, for our comely parts have no need: but God hath tempered the body together, having given more abundant honor to that part which lacked.

Verse 25, That there should be no schism in the body; but that the members should have the same care one for another.

Verse 26, And whether one member suffer, all the members suffer with it; or one member be honored, all the members rejoice with it.

Verse 27, now ye are the body of Christ, and members in particular.

This explanation we see in first Corinthians is self-explanatory and it doesn't require being a scientist to understand it, the church of the Lord Jesus Christ is not a physical building, the building is where all the corporate body meets for fellowship.

The church of the Lord Jesus Christ is made up of individual members, so the traditional philosophy that I'm going to church, is totally wrong, we are the church, and members in particular.

One of the things that happens when we are spiritually born again, and we become a new creation, it is for the sole purpose of becoming the body of Christ.

His earthly corporate body, where not only does he inhabit every believer, but when we praise and worship him he makes himself present, for he said that when two or three are gathered together in my name there am I in the midst of them.

This corporate body can meet anywhere, in a big auditorium, in a big stadium, in a designated building, in a particular home, anywhere where two or more are gathered there is the corporate body of the Lord Jesus Christ.

God is no respecter of persons every one of us believers is considered the corporate body of the Lord Jesus Christ, with different functions, with different callings, and different anointing.

And we cannot have preferences, in choosing to which of the members I'm going to get closer to, and this is very clear between verse 15, and, 17.

On verse 27, now ye are the body of Christ, and members in particular.

Now let's look at who placed the members in the body?

On verse 18, But now hath God set the members every one of them in the body, as it hath pleased him.

Now according to God's will in God's word, let's look at the members that are more important in the body.

Verse 23, And those members of the body, which we think to be less honorable, upon these we bestow more abundant honor; and our uncomely parts have more abundant comeliness.

This is very powerful according to the word of God, we were inserted into Christ's body, and we became the member that God wanted us to be in the body, handpicked by God himself, he called us, he chose us, he sealed us, he gave us the new birth, and he personally set us in the body as it pleased him, this is shouting good news right now. Hallelujah.

On verse 25, we see God's original intent in selecting, in choosing, and in inserting us, and making us the members of the body as it pleased him, that there should be no schism in the body; but that the members should have the same care one for another.

So if you are in a local church and the pastor does not recognize you, or elders do not like you, who for some reason they had been giving you an opportunity to minister through your gifts in the body, be patient and pray for them because they have not yet seen God's calling upon your life.

As a member of Christ's body our self-worth, our self-esteem, our myself value, should be at all time high because of who we are, because who chose us, because who inserted us in the body, and regardless of how much, or how little they acknowledge us, we are still God's, we're washed in the blood, we are sealed with the Holy Spirit of promise, and we have been born in a spiritual family called the body of the Lord Jesus Christ.

I am a member of Christ's body and no devil in hell, or human on this earth, can change the handpicked member of Christ's body, just be sure that you are born again Christian.

Therefore I am, what God says, that I am.

GOD SAYS, THAT I AM,
(A TEMPLE OF THE HOLY SPIRIT)

In the epistle of Paul to second Corinthians chapter 6:14, 18 Be ye not unequally yoked together with unbelievers: for what fellowship hath righteousness with unrighteousness? And what communion hath light with darkness?

Verse 15, And what Concord has Christ with Be-li-al? Or what part hath he that believeth with an infidel?

Verse 16, Or what agreement hath the temple of God with idols? For ye are the temple of the living God; as God hath said, I will dwell in them, and walk in them; and I will be their God, and they shall be my people.

Verse 17, wherefore come out from among them, and be ye separate, saith the Lord, and touch not the unclean thing; and I will receive you.

Verse 18, And will be a father unto you, and ye shall be my sons and daughters, saith the Lord Almighty.

On these verses it is evident that God does not want us to be in a relationship with a person that is not saved, it's a very clear evident what God calls the believer, versus the nonbeliever, and although it may sound like we're judging somebody else, we are only quoting the word of Almighty God, and how many of you know, that he is right and we are wrong.

God calls us, the believer's (righteousness), we have already explained that we are the righteousness of God in Christ, and God calls the unbeliever unrighteousness.

God calls us, the believer's (light), and God calls the unbelievers (darkness).

God calls us, the believer's (Christ's), and God calls the unbelievers Be-li-al.

God calls us, the believer's (Believers), and God calls the unbelievers infidels.

God calls us, the believer's (temple of God), and God calls the unbelievers idols.

God calls us, the believer's (his dwelling place), (and walk in us).

And God said, that (he would be our God).

And God said, that (we would be his people).

And the prerequisite for us to develop our identity is found on verse 17, and he says, for us to come out from among them, and to be separate, and touch not any unclean thing, and he promised to receive us and make us his own.

And God said that he would be our father, and that we would be his sons and daughters.

So as long as we're quoting what God says, are we being boastful? Or are we being biblical? You be the judge, I've made up my mind to say what God says, to believe what God says, to stand up on what God says, and that settles it. Regardless of other people's opinion, and with all their due respect, their views, their ways, and their value system, means absolutely nothing to me, only what God says am I interested in, and that is what I'm going to confess, that is what I'm going to believe, and that is what I'm going to live by.

God says that we ARE, Righteousness, God says that we ARE, light, God says that we ARE, Christ's= Anointed, God says that we

ARE, believers, God says that we ARE, Temple of God where his Holy Spirit lives, God says that we ARE, his dwelling place, God said that he would walk in us, God said he would be our God, God said we would be his people, and lastly God said we would be his sons and daughters.

According to God's holy word, according to God's holy Constitution, according to God's New Testament and the new birth that I have received, (I am what God says that I am.)

GOD SAYS, THAT I AM, (AN AMBASSADOR FOR CHRIST)

In the epistle of Paul to the Corinthians chapter 5:20 Now then we are ambassadors for Christ, as though God did beseech you by as: we pray you in Christ's stead, be ye reconciled to God.

Now on this teaching as we progress and move forward, it is extremely important to understand, that this is the identity that God wanted us to have, nothing more, nothing less.

What does it mean to be an (ambassador) for Christ?

I obviously had to look up the word in the Webster comprehensive dictionary, and it was extraordinary what I found.

Number one, an accredited diplomatic agent of the highest rank.

Number two, an appointed representative of one government or state.

Number three, to represent a government or state at a particular function.

Number four, any personal representative or messenger.

Number five, an ambassador- at- large, an ambassador accredited to no specific country or government.

Number six, a goodwill ambassador, is a person traveling in a foreign country to promote friendly relations and understanding.

Now these are the earthly interpretations of an appointed task to a specific individual for the representation of that country, state, or local government.

Now this ambassador does not speak of his own, but he only speaks what he is told to speak, regardless of how he feels, regardless of what others say about him, regardless of the views and ways of other people, he has been given a job title, and a message to share with, or to communicate to other people, and in other countries.

Can we truly imagine what it is to be called an ambassador for Christ, given to us by the Creator of the sun, the moon, the stars, and every created being?

Do we understand? And can we truly imagine? That this is an accredited diplomatic agent of the highest rank.

That we have been chosen by the creator of the universe to be his representatives of heaven upon earth.

That we are heaven's representatives here on earth of the mysteries of God through the revelation AL knowledge of his word towards people.

That we are to represent the spiritual kingdom of Almighty God as an ambassador for Christ, as though God himself was making his reply through us, and that he himself has given us the ministry of reconciliation.

Can you really imagine this God-given calling, and the power that we have been given to reconcile human beings with God.

It's like the goodwill ambassador traveling to a foreign country to promote friendly relationships and understanding about their maker, Redeemer, deliverer, baptizer, and Commissioner.

Isn't this something that is mind-boggling? Isn't this incomprehensible? It took me almost 10 to 15 years to truly understand, and internalize such a powerful message.

In the letter of Paul to the Ephesians chapter 6:19, 20 And for me, that utterance may be given to me, that I may open my mouth boldly, to make known the mysteries of the gospel,

Verse 20, for which I am an ambassador in bonds: that therein I may speak boldly, as I ought to speak.

Paul was constantly praying that the God of heaven through the Holy Spirit would give him the boldness, so that he would open up his mouth boldly, to make known the mysteries of the gospel, for which he was an ambassador in bonds, and the same spirit will give him the boldness to speak as he ought to.

As ambassadors for Christ that we all are, we need to develop a life of prayer, that God may give us the divine Revelation in the mystery of this beautiful gospel that has been bought and paid for by the blood of Jesus Christ.

And sometimes when our self-worth is down, when our self-value is constantly being attacked by the enemy, and our self-esteem has been used and abused and taken advantage of, we may realize that we are not what we feel, we are not what we think, that we are not what other people tell us we are, we are only what DOTH SAYETH God in his holy word.

Now an ambassador speaks only what he has heard his superior God the Holy Spirit say.

And an ambassador represents only another kingdom, a spiritual kingdom.

And an ambassador is delegated authority to decide.

And an ambassador for Christ has the God-given power to act upon a situation.

And an ambassador for Christ has a heavenly given protection.

And an ambassador for Christ looks good and dresses good.

And an ambassador for Christ should not be broken, but sufficient for everything.

And an ambassador for Christ has guardian angels encamping around them all the time.

And an ambassador for Christ should live in a good home.

And an ambassador for Christ should have a good car to get around in.

And an ambassador for Christ should have private transportation to fly with.

And lastly an ambassador for Christ should have a healthy self-esteem, self-worth, and self-value, rooted and grounded in the only covenant that will not pass away, the New Testament. To God be the glory great things he has done in the person of Jesus Christ, Amen.

I AM A CHOSEN GENERATION, A ROYAL PRIESTHOOD, A HOLY NATION, A PECULIAR PEOPLE, AND TO SHOW FORTH THE PRAISES OF HIM

God says, that I am, a chosen generation:
God says, that I am, a royal priesthood:
God says, that I am, a holy nation:
God says, that I am, a peculiar people:
God says, that I am, to show forth the praises of him:

In the first epistle of Peter chapter 2:9,10 But ye are a chosen generation, a royal priesthood, an holy nation, a peculiar people; that ye should show forth the praises of him who has called you out of darkness into his marvelous light.

Verse 10, which in time past were not a people, but are now the people of God, Which had not obtained mercy, but now have obtained mercy.

In order to understand how blessed we Christians are, we need to understand where our blessing is coming from, when God says that we are a chosen generation, a royal priesthood, a holy nation, a peculiar people, to show forth the praises of him who called us out of darkness into his marvelous light, we need to understand that through this blood line this marvelous inheritance has come upon us, so we have to start with Abraham the father of many nations.

Please understand from the loins of Abraham came the children of Israel, all the Arabs in the world, and every Gentile that has made Jesus Christ his Lord and Savior.

The word Gentile is any human being that is not of the bloodline of the Jewish people.

But when we look in Galatians 3:29 and if ye be Christ's, then are ye Abraham's seed, and heirs according to the promise.

The prerequisite here is, if ye be Christ's? Then are ye Abraham's seed, and heirs according to the promise, whether Jew, Gentile or any other culture.

In the epistle of Paul to the Romans chapter 11:1, 36 We will start at Verse 13 But I am speaking to you who are Gentiles. Inasmuch then as I am an apostle of Gentiles, I magnify my ministry,

Verse 14, If somehow I my move to jealousy my fellow countrymen and save some of them.

Verse 15, For if their rejection be the reconciliation of the world, what will their acceptance be but life from the dead?

Verse 16, and is the first piece of dough be holy, the lump is also; and if the root be holy, the branches are to.

Verse 17, But if some of the branches were broken off, and you, being a wild olive, were grafted in among them and became partakers with them of the rich root of the olive tree,

Verse 18, do not be arrogant toward the branches; but if you are arrogant, remember that it is not you who supports the root, but the root supports you.

Verse 19, you will say then, "Branches were broken off so that I might be crafted in."

Verse 20, quite right, they were broken off for their unbelief, but you stand by your faith. Do not be conceited, but fear;

Verse 21, for if God did not spare the natural branches, neither will he spare you.

Verse 22, behold then the kindness and severity of God; to those who fell, severity, but to you, God's kindness, if you continue in his kindness; otherwise you also will be cut off.

Verse 23, and they also, if they do not continue in their unbelief, will be grafted in; for God is able to graft them in again.

Verse 24, for if you were cut off from what is by nature a wild olive tree, and were grafted contrary to nature into a cultivated olive tree, how much more shall these who are the natural branches be grafted into their own olive tree?

Verse 25, For I do not want you, brethren, to be uninformed of this mystery, this should be wise in your own estimation, that a partial hardening has happened to Israel until the fullness of the Gentiles has come in;

Verse 26, and thus all Israel will be saved; just as it is written, "The deliverer will come from Zion, he will remove ungodliness from Jacob."

Verse 27, "and this is my covenant with them, when I take away their sins.

On these verses is very clear that the apostle Paul is talking to the Gentiles, for he was the apostle to the Gentiles with the divine revelation of the gospel, and we are considered a wild Olive. On Verse 17 we see that the Jewish people are considered the branches that were broken off, and they were broken off because of unbelief, and that the wild Olive (Gentiles) was grafted in to the rich root of the Olive tree, because of our faith in Jesus Christ, and because of that, he does not want us to be conceited or proud full against the branches.

On verse 22, we see the severity of God to those who fell, and the goodness of God to those who by faith in Jesus Christ persevere in kindness.

On verse 24 we the Gentiles were grafted contrary to nature into a cultivated olive tree, so this makes us in the natural descendants with the people of Israel and joint heirs with the Commonwealth of Israel.

On verse 25 the apostle Paul here is saying that we should not be ignorant or uninformed of this mystery, and that this partial hardening has happened to Israel until the fullness of the Gentiles has come.

Then on verse 26 all Israel will be saved and all the ungodliness from the house of Jacob will be removed,

and he will take away their sins, for the New Testament is his covenant with them.

This is why in Galatians chapter 4:4,7 But when the fullness of time came, (the fullness of time came, means the number six dispensation, the dispensation of grace, from the birth of Christ up until now,) God sent forth his son, born of a woman, born under the law,

Verse five, in order that he might redeem those who were under the law, that we might receive the adoption as sons.

Verse six, and because you are sons, God has sent forth the Spirit of his son into our hearts, crying, "Abba! Father!"

Verse seven, Therefore you are no longer a slave, but a son; and if a son, then an heir through God.

God has sent his Spirit upon our hearts thereby giving us the opportunity to cry Abba! Father! Because he has already redeemed us, by the precious blood of his son born of a woman under the law, therefore we have been adopted as sons of God, therefore we are no longer slaves but we are sons, and heirs with God.

In the epistle of Paul to the Ephesians chapter 2:12 remember that you were at that time separate from Christ, excluded from the Commonwealth of Israel, and strangers of the covenants of promise, having no hope and without God in the world.

Verse 13, But now in Christ Jesus you who formerly were far off have been brought near, by the blood of Christ.

Verse 14, For he himself is our peace, who made both groups into one, and broke down the barrier of the dividing wall,

Verse 15, by abolishing in his flesh the enmity, which is the law of commandments contained in ordinances, that in himself he might make two into one new man, thus establishing peace.

Verse 16, and might reconcile them both in one body to God through the cross, by it having put to death the enmity.

Verse 17, And he came and preach peace to you who were far away, and peace to those who were near;

Verse 18, for through him we both have our access in one spirit to the father.

Verse 19, So then you are no longer strangers and aliens, but you are fellow citizens with the Saints, and are of God's household.

When both Jews and Gentiles get on their knees and cry out to God and receive Jesus Christ of Nazareth into their hearts we become a brand-new creation.

No longer separate from Christ, excluded from the Commonwealth of Israel, and strangers of the covenants, having no hope and without God in the world.

But we are now brought near thanks to the blood of Jesus Christ on the cross, which broke down the barriers of the dividing walls, by abolishing in his flesh the enmity which is the law and commandments contained in ordinances.

So God in his redemptive program wanted to make out of the Jews and the Gentiles one new man, establishing peace.

He wanted to reconcile them both Jews and the Gentiles into one body by the cross, and by it having put to death the enmity.

So through Christ we both could have access in one spirit to the father.

On verse 19, so then we are no longer strangers and aliens, but we are fellow citizens with the Saints, and we are of God's household, hallelujah.

Oh thank you Jesus, through your precious blood, out of both Jews and Gentiles, you have abolished the enmity between us, and you have brought down the dividing walls, and you have given to us by one spirit the privilege of common union with the father.

Oh hallelujah, when first Peter 2:9, 10 said that we were a chosen generation, a Royal priesthood, a holy nation, a peculiar people, to show forth the praises of him who called us out of darkness into his wonderful light, he was not exaggerating, in another translation of the word it says, that you may proclaim the excellency of him who has called you of darkness into his marvelous light.

So in the epistle of Paul to the Romans chapter 8:16, 17 The spirit himself bears witness with our spirit that we are children of God,

Verse 17, and if children, heirs also, heirs of God and fellow heirs with Christ, if indeed we suffer with him in order that we may also be glorified with him.

Every child of Almighty God, is an heir with God, and fellow heir with Christ, his spirit bears witness with our spirit that we are children of God, if we suffer with him so that we may be glorified with him, for our destiny in Christ is a glorified body in heaven.

And just as we read in Galatians chapter 3:29 and because we are Christ's, we are of Abraham's seed, and heirs according to the promise, God gave Abraham.

When we look in Genesis chapter 17:4,8 "As for me, behold, my covenant is with you, and you shall be the father of a multitude of nations,

Verse five, "No longer shall your name be Abram;

For I will make you the father multitude of nations.

Verse six, "And I will make you exceedingly fruitful, and I will make nations of you, and Kings shall come forth from you.

Verse seven, "And I will establish my covenant between me and you and your descendants after you throughout their generations for an everlasting covenant, to be God to you and to your descendants after you.

Verse eight "And I will give to you and to your descendants after you, the land of your sojourning's, all the land of Canaan, for an everlasting possession; and I will be there God."

These are powerful promises that are given to anyone who makes Jesus Christ their Lord and Savior, through the spiritual side, and through the physical side we are blessed.

Everything that Abraham had was passed on to his seed and 42 generations later the word says in the epistle to the Galatians chapter 3:16 Now the promises were spoken to Abraham and to his seed. He does not say, "And to seeds," as referring to many, but rather to one, "And to your seed," that is, Christ.

In this spiritual life we are a new creature, having a new life, with the seed of Almighty God in us, being children of God and descendants of God.

But in the natural if ye be Christ's, then we are the seed of Abraham, and heirs according to the promise, that God gave Abraham, so it is to our best interest to find out what God promised Abraham.

As we just read in Genesis 17:4, 8 God said as for me, behold my covenant is with you, so that the covenant was in Abraham, through Christ the covenant is with us, then he promised him he was going to be the father of multitude of nations, through Jesus Christ of Nazareth, any nation in the world that believes in the Lordship of Jesus Christ is a grafted into that blessing, and through Christ they also become an heir and joint heir with Christ, of that Abraham's covenant.

God no longer wanted Abram to be his name, but Abraham because he was making him into the father of multitude of nations.

And that multitude of nations is us, every gentile around the world that repents and believes in Jesus Christ as Lord, is one of those multitudes of nations.

And he promised to make him exceedingly fruitful, and that he would make nations out of Abraham, and Kings would come forth from him.

God in his covenant even went to the extent of changing his name.

So through the seed of Abraham which is Christ we all can expect the blessings of Abraham, to come upon our lives

Now one of these promises was to make him exceedingly fruitful, then that exceedingly fruitful promise is applicable to us, we should all be exceedingly fruitful, and then later on I will address why a lot of Christians are not exceedingly fruitful.

Now he also said that King's will come forth from Abraham's seed, now in the old covenant which is the 5th dispensation of law, we saw many Kings like the judges, like Saul, like David, like Solomon, that rained in Israel, but in the new covenant number 6th dispensation, from Pentecost to the rapture where we are now, the dispensation of grace, the dispensation of the unmerited favor, which is a spiritual dispensation, we are Kings over the spiritual realm that our elder brother defeated for us, and handed over to us the victory, but why do you think that the Bible says that we are more than conquerors, because Jesus conquered principalities, powers, and rulers of this dark age, and made a show of them openly triumphing over them on the cross. And this is found in the epistle of Paul to the Colossians chapter 2:15.

And by defeating Death, hell, the grave, and all those principalities and powers and rulers which administered fear to all humanity, and in the gospel of Luke chapter 10:19 "behold, I have given you authority to tread upon serpents and scorpions, and over all the power of the enemy, and nothing shall injure you.

He not only made us free, he not only broke every yoke of bondage in our lives, he gave us a brand-new life, he baptized us in the Holy Spirit, and he delegated that authority to tread upon serpents and scorpions and over all the power of the enemy, this makes us Kings, rulers, and a victorious church overcoming all the wiles of the enemy, thanks to the delegated supernatural authority against all the power of the enemy against us.

You See My Brother Why We Are a Chosen Generation, Why We Are Royal Priesthood, Why We Are Peculiar People, to Show

Forth in the Spirit Realm the Praises of Him Who Called Us Out Of Darkness into His Marvelous Light, hallelujah.

Know Jesus Christ is the King, this is why it says that he is the King of Kings and he is the Lord of Lords.

And in Genesis chapter 13:1, 2 So Abram went up from Egypt to the neget, he and his wife and all that belonged to him; and Lot with him.

Verse two, Now Abram was very rich in livestock, in silver and in gold.

Now livestock is the equivalent to every material thing that we will ever need, And Silver, is the equivalent to Intelligence, Proverbs 16:16 And Gold, is the equivalent t of Wisdom Proverbs 16:16.

Now in Romans chapter 4:13 For the promise to Abraham or to his descendants that he would be heir of the world was not through the law, but to the righteousness of faith.

That is you and I, in whose righteousness was attributed to us by faith in Jesus Christ, which we have already read.

Now in Genesis 12:1,3 Now the Lord said to Abram, go forth from your country, and from your relatives and from your father's house, to the land which I will show you;

Verse two And I will make you a great nation, and I will bless you, and make your name great; and so you shall be a blessing;

Verse three And I will bless those who bless you, and the one who curses you I will curse.

And in you all the families of the earth shall be blessed,"
Because we are the seed of Abraham, anybody that curses us, is cursing Abraham, and in so doing God himself will Curse Him. Every blessing that God poured out to Abraham because we are of his seed; it belongs to us, thanks to the shed blood of the new covenant on the cross.

And in Genesis chapter 25:7, 8 And these are all the years of Abraham's life that he lived, 175 years.

Verse eight, And Abraham breathed his last and died in a ripe old age, an old man and satisfied with life; and he was gathered to his people.

A long life Abraham lived, a long life we should live.
Abraham had a ripe old age, and a ripe old age is what we should have.
He reached his old age satisfied with life; we should reach our old age and be satisfied with life and every one of God's blessings upon our lives.
And all of this that you have been reading my friend, is God's generational blessings, from Abraham to Jesus Christ 42 exact generations, and when we got born again, and when we got saved, we were grafted into this wonderful family, thereby becoming an heir and a joint heir with Christ, hallelujah, thank you Jesus. All of Abraham's blessings belong to us, and we are that chosen generation, we are Royal priesthood, we are holy nation, we are that peculiar people, chosen by God himself, elected by God himself, predestined by God himself, to be the air of such wonderful blessings.

So we are God's children with supernatural and heavenly blessings upon our lives, and thanks to the Lord Jesus Christ, we are of the seed of Abraham and Ayers according to the promise.

As we take in all of this wonderful information, and we pass it from our head into our hearts, and we meditate on this generational blessings coming from God's New Testament, which is God's holy will, sometimes I wonder why it costs us so much to believe our inheritance. (I am) what God says (I am), and (that settles it):

God says, (that I have), (What he says I have)

In Romans chapter 12:3 For I say, through the grace given unto me, every man that is among you, not to think of himself more highly than he ought to think; but to think soberly, according as God has dealt to every man the measure of faith.

GOD SAYS, I HAVE A FULL ARMOR, (FAITH), (BELIEVE), (CONVICTIONS)

The enemy constantly attacks are mind, throwing fiery darts against it through unworthy thoughts, negative thoughts so that our hope would be in the gutter, thereby causing question marks in our mind contrary to the facts, which is why we need to realize that we have a shield of faith that the Bible talks about.

> **In the epistle of Paul to the Ephesians chapter 6:11, 18 Put on the full armor of God, that you may be able to stand firm against the schemes of the devil.**
>
> **Verse 12, For our struggle is not against flesh and blood, but against the rulers, against the powers, against the world forces of this darkness, against the spiritual forces of wickedness in the heavenly places.**
>
> **Verse 13, Therefore, take up the full armor of God, that you may be able to resist and the evil day, and having done everything, to stand firm.**
>
> **Verse 14, Stand firm therefore, having girded your loins with truth, and having put on the breastplate of righteousness,**
>
> **Verse 15, and having shod your feet with the preparation of the gospel of peace; the**

Verse 16, in addition to all, taking up the shield of faith with which you will be able to extinguish all the flaming missiles of the evil one.

Verse 17, and take the helmet of salvation, and the sword of the spirit, which is the word of God.

When the Bible says put on the full armor of God that you may be able to stand firm against the schemes of the devil, he was advising us to put on everything we have been reading on this book in our hearts about who we truly are in Christ, our identity in Christ, are supernatural rebirth in Christ, God's supernatural seed in us, the fact that we are members of Christ's body, and that we are Royal priesthood chosen by God thanks to the shed blood of Jesus Christ on the cross.

And unless we take this information and pass it from our head into our hearts the enemy will constantly be throwing fiery darts to cause us to think that we are worthless, to cause us to think we are powerless, to cause us to think we are no good, taking every one of our failures and throwing it against our face, and even the smallest mistakes we make causing us to think that because of those mistakes, everything we have ever worked for in the area family, in the area of ministry, in the area of business, it's over, and is nothing but a lie from the pit of hell.

Now when the Bible says put on the full armor, this means that some people have put on, or have used parts of the armor but not the full armor, thereby being defeated in some areas of their lives.

Our struggle is in our mind where the enemy is constantly bombarding us, and constantly reminding us of our failures.

And after 30 years of walking with the Lord I have come to the conclusion that our positional relationship with God never changes, it is our progressive relationship to God through the Fellowship of the Holy Spirit that is hindered when we sin.

And as we already said as we confess our faults he is faithful and just to forgive us and to cleanse us from all unrighteousness, thereby restoring our fellowship with the father.

We should always gird our loins with the truth, which what it really means is walking in truthfulness.

To put on of the breastplate of righteousness, which is to take the righteousness teaching we have already read in this book and pass it into our hearts.

Having shod our feet with the preparation of the gospel of peace, means to always be ready to take this gospel of peace, and revelation AL knowledge anywhere we go.

And to take up the shield of faith, it really means to keep up constantly our level of faith which was deposited within us, Romans 12:3. Which means not to think of yourselves more highly than you ought to think, but to think soberly according to the measure of faith that God has dealt to every man?

Everything that is in the holy word of God has to be received by faith, because it is by faith, and it is through faith that we receive all of his promises, and we have a shield of faith that we may be able to extinguish all the flaming missiles of the evil one.

Now obviously you know that the evil one is not throwing flaming physical missiles at us, but his flaming missiles are coming against us through our patterns of thought, through feelings of unworthiness, through feelings of rejection, through feelings of abandonment, through feelings of no acceptance, and ultimately getting us to be depressed, and if we do not gird our loins with God's truth and we believe this lie he will tell us to end our lives.

Now we have already talked about the helmet of our salvation, and we have already talked about the breastplate of righteousness, and we already talked about the preparation of our feet with the gospel of peace, and we already talked about the shield of faith.

As you very well may now there are no physical sword of the spirit, but there is a physical word of Almighty God, and as we try to discover our identity in Christ, our rights and privileges in Christ, and our God-given power in Christ, then we are decreeing the word of Almighty God. And inheriting everything that God through Christ purchased for us. And that is our sword of the spirit, the decreeing of his holy word.

Number one, as we discover the word of God.
Number two, as we read the word of God.
Number three, as we believe the word of God.
Number four, as we meditate on the word of God.
Number five, as we pass this information into our hearts.
Number six, and as we start acting upon this holy word of God.
Number seven, it starts becoming Rhema in our hearts.

Our heavenly father did not go to the extreme of taking up flesh to himself and coming in the person of Jesus Christ, to die by the hands of the people he had created on a brutal cross, shedding innocent blood, thereby purchasing us from the gates of hell, defeating the devil himself, and giving us the victory that we may go around with a poor old me syndrome, which I will never get anywhere is mentality, and with the mentality that the devil is out to get me.

He made us a victorious Christian because he saved us and he is now living in us by the power of the precious Holy Spirit.

GOD SAYS, THAT I HAVE, (A NEW LIFE)

In the gospel of John chapter 10:10 "The thief comes only to steal, and kill, and destroy; I came that they might have life, and might have it abundantly.

It is imperative that we know why the thief came into this world, this is why it's so vitally important that we internalize everything we are reading and make it our own, because the thief only came to steal it from us, and to destroy our lives, but thanks' be to God that Jesus Christ came to give us life and life more abundant.

When Jesus Christ of Nazareth entered our being he brought in with himself the ZOE kind of life which is the life of God, and we have that Kind of life in us right now.

GOD SAYS, THAT I HAVE, (A DIVINED NATURE)

In the second epistle Peter chapter 1:2,9 Grace and peace be multiplied to you in the knowledge of God and of Jesus our Lord;

Verse three, seeing that his divine power has granted to us everything pertaining to life and godliness, through the true knowledge of him who called us by his own glory and excellence.

Verse four, For by these he has granted to us his precious and magnificent promises, in order in that by them you might become partakers of the divine nature, having escaped the corruption that is in the world by lust.

His divine power has granted to us everything pertaining to life and godliness, and it is only through the true knowledge of Jesus Christ who called us by his own glory and excellence.

Knowing that by these he has granted to us those precious and magnificent promises, in order that by them we might become partakers of the divine nature. In the here and now.

GOD SAYS, THAT I HAVE, (A CITIZENSHIP IN HEAVEN)

In the epistle of Paul to the Ephesians chapter 2:19 So then you are no longer strangers and aliens, but you are fellow citizens with the Saints, and are of God's household.

I have a brand-new family, I have a heavenly father, I'm no longer a stranger or an alien, I'm no longer an illegal alien, but I'm a fellow citizen with the Saints and I am a member of God's household.

In the letter of Paul to the Philippians chapter 3:20 For our citizenship is in heaven, from which also we eagerly wait for a Savior, the Lord Jesus Christ;

Verse 21, who will transform the body of our humble estate into conformity with the body of his glory, by the exertion of the power that he has even to subject all things to himself.

Thank God that our citizenship is in heaven, and we are definitely heaven bound.

We have a new life, we have a new divine nature, we have everything pertaining to life and godliness, we have precious and magnificent promises, we have become partakers of his divine nature, we have a brand-new family, we have a brand-new father, we are no longer aliens, we have a citizenship with the Saints in heaven, and we have become members of God's household, and we have the promise of the transformation of our humble estate, into the conformity of his glorious body, hallelujah.

We have what God says we have.

GOD SAYS, THAT I HAVE, (BEAN MADE FREE)

In the epistle of Paul to the Galatians chapter 5:1 It was for freedom that Christ set us free; therefore keep standing firm and do not be subject again to a yoke of slavery.

It was for freedom that Jesus Christ set us all free, thank God that we are free, thank God that we live in a free country, thank God that we no longer need to be enslaved to anything, or to anyone, thank God for freedom of speech.

Therefore I'm going to keep standing firm, I'm going to keep confessing the word of God, I'm going to keep renewing my mind with the word of God, thank God he has made me a free moral agent, who possesses a soul and lives in a body.

Thank God I have freedom in my soul, thank God I have freedom in my mind, thank God I have freedom in my body, thank God I have freedom in my home, thank God I have freedom with my relationships, and thank God I will never be bound ever again, from whom the son of God sets free, is free in deed, hallelujah.

GOD SAYS, THAT I HAVE,
(HIS LEADERSHIP FOR TRIUMPH)

In the second epistle of Paul to the Corinthians 2:14 But thanks be to God, who always leads us in his triumph in Christ, and manifests through us the sweet aroma of the knowledge of him in every place.

Every Christian has the assurance that God will always lead us in triumph in Jesus Christ.

In no other faith, in no other religion, in any other believe system, do human beings have an assurance of victory.

And then manifests the sweet aroma of this wonderful knowledge in every place that we go.

And we have the assurance of victory.

In the acts of the apostles chapter 1:8 but you shall receive power when the Holy Spirit has come upon you; and you shall be my witnesses both in Jerusalem, and in all Judea and Samaria, and even to the remotest part of earth.

Every born-again believer that has received the baptism in the Holy Spirit as we just read, has the power to cast out devils, to tread over serpents and scorpions and all the power of the enemy, this is in the gospel of Luke 10:19.

You and I have received the power, the delegated authority, to use the name of Jesus against all of the oppressing attacks of the enemy against our lives, or anyone we come in contact with, Jesus

Christ does not lie, and his word does not lie, and he is not a man that he should repent, because he has established his new covenant for us to believe and act upon.

If Jesus said it, you can believe it, you can act upon it, and it will come to pass, thank you Lord.

Every time we read the word of God which is the Bible, God's covenant, God's New Testament, God's holy will, the inheritance of God for his people, we are his people those of us that has received Jesus Christ as our Savior and Lord are the recipients of this beautiful inheritance, God's holy word is our inheritance, and every time we read it we should believe with all our hearts what we are reading, was written for our benefit.

So when we read the holy word of God we are reading God's commitment to us, God's covenant with us, God's New Testament for us, with God's will written on his word for us, that we may inherit the blessings bought and paid for by the blood of Jesus Christ on the cross.

GOD SAYS, THAT I HAVE, (A HIGH PRIEST, AND A MEDIATOR)

In the epistle written to the Hebrews chapter 9:11, 17 But when Christ appeared as a high priest of the good things to come, he entered through the greater and more perfect tabernacle, not made with hands, that is to say, not of his creation;

Verse 12, and not through the blood of goats and calves, but through his own blood, he entered the holy place once for all, having obtained eternal redemption.

Verse 13, For if the blood of goats and bulls and the ashes on a heifer sprinkling those who have been defiled, sanctify for the cleansing of the flesh,

Verse 14, how much more will the blood of Christ, who through the eternal Spirit offered himself without blemish to God; cleanse your conscience from dead works to serve the living God?

Verse 15, But for this reason he is the mediator of the new covenant, in order that since death has taken place for the redemption of the transgressions that were committed under the first covenant, those who have been called may receive the promise of the eternal inheritance.

Verse 16, For where a covenant is, there must of necessity be the death of the one who made it.

Verse 17, For a covenant is valid only when men are dead, for it is never enforced while the one who made it lives.

On these six versus the explanation is so powerful and so clear that our covenant, that our New Testament covenants, was left to us by Jesus Christ himself.

Notice all the past tense words that are being said here on verse 11, but when Christ appeared as a high priest of the good things to come, and those good things to come you are already reading in this book, which is what the testator left you in his testament, his redemptive blood shed on the cross, and he went into the holy of holies in heavenly tabernacle and there he sprinkled it on the mercy seat on the altar, and obtained once and for all eternal redemption.

We have been eternally redeemed, purchased, not through the blood of calves and goats, but through his precious blood that through his eternal spirit offered himself without blemish to God, thereby cleansing our consciousness, that we may serve the living God.

That is why he and only he is the mediator of a new covenant between God Almighty and human beings so that we who are called may receive the promise of eternal inheritance.

And the fact that he died on the cross, was buried in a tomb, rose up from the dead, and sat himself at the right end of the father, as the mediator, a heavenly lawyer in our behalf, and with his death burial and resurrection fulfilled his calling.

We are the recipients, in the benefactors of the new covenant.

So we have a new covenant, called the New Testament, found in the word of God, which is called the Holy Scriptures of God, the holy Bible written that we may know the will of God for every single area of our lives.

GOD SAYS, THAT I HAVE, (A NEW COVENANT)

In Hebrews chapter 8:1,6,13 Now the main point in what has been said is this: we have such a high priest, who has taken his seat at the right hand of the throne of the Majesty in the heavens,

Verse two, a minister in the sanctuary, and in the true tabernacle, which the Lord pitched, not man.

Verse six, But now he has obtained a more excellent ministry, by as much as he is also the mediator of a better covenant, which has been enacted on better promises.

Verse seven, For if that first covenant had been faultless, there would have been no occasion sought for a second.

Verse eight, For finding fault with them, he says, "Behold, days are coming, saith the Lord, when I will perfect a new covenant with the house of Israel and with the house of Judah;

Verse nine, Not like the covenant which I made with their fathers on the day when I took them by the hand to lead them out of the land of Egypt; for they did not continue in my covenant, and I did not care for them, saith the Lord.

Verse 10, "For this is the covenant that I will make with the house of Israel, after those days, saith the Lord: I will put my laws into their minds, and I will write them upon their hearts. And I will be there God, and they shall be my people.

Verse 11, "and they shall not teach everyone his fellow citizen, and every one of his brother, saying, 'Know the Lord,' for all shall know me, from the least to the greatest of them.

Verse 12, "For I will be merciful to their iniquities, and I will remember their sins no more."

Verse 13, When he said, "A new covenant," He has made the first obsolete. But whatever is becoming obsolete and growing old is ready to disappear.

Not only had the Lord promised a seed to Abraham, but he underscored it by swearing by himself, for no one could be greater than God.

Thus the writer encourages the faith of believers who may be sluggish in their endeavors for Christ and his kingdom. He calls believers to imitate those who "through faith and patience inherit the promises." A look at Abraham, who was ordered to sacrifice his only son Isaac, provides the ultimate example of faith in God's covenant promises.

All Abraham had was the word of promise in some 30 or 40 years of trusting God's word.

Then the Lord strengthened his original promise by swearing an oath by himself.

What a ministry of affirmation, how could it be otherwise, since the Lord our God is so gracious and faithful, so that the word of promise always can be trusted?

It is absolutely imperative we understand that in this new dispensation of grace, of the unmerited favor towards Jews as well as Gentiles, that God himself is waiting until the fullness of the Gentiles has come.

GOD SAYS, THAT I HAVE, (BEEN GRAFTED IN TO THE RICH ROOT)

In Romans chapter 11:17 but if some of the branches were broken off, and you, being a wild Olive, were grafted in among them and became partakers with them of the rich root of the Olive tree.

Verse 18, do not be arrogant toward the branches; but if you are arrogant, remember that it is not you who supports the root, but the root supports you.

Just as we said earlier every Gentile around the world that has received Jesus Christ of Nazareth, have been grafted into the rich root which is the Commonwealth of Israel, which is the seed of Abraham, which is the natural Jewish family, thanks be to God for this new covenant.

In Romans chapter 11:23 And they also, if they do not continue in their unbelief, will be grafted in; for God is able to graft them in again.

Verse 25, For I do not want you, brethren, to be uninformed of this mystery, this should be wise in your own estimation, that a partial hardening has happened to Israel until the fullness of the Gentiles has come in;

Verse 26, and that all Israel will be saved; just as it is written, "the deliverer will come from Zion, he will remove ungodliness from Jacob,"

Verse 27 And this is my covenant with them, when I take away their sins."

Now In Jeremiah chapter 31:32, 34 not like the covenant which I may with their fathers in the day I took them by the hand to bring them out of the land of Egypt, my covenant which they broke, although I was a husband to them, declares the Lord.

Verse 33, "But this is the covenant which I will make with the house of Israel after those days," declares the Lord, "I will put my law within them, and on their hearts I will write it; and I will be there God, and they shall be my people.

Verse 34, "And they shall not teach again, each man his neighbor and each man his brother, saying, Know the Lord,' for they shall all know me, from the least of them to the greatest of them," declares the Lord, "for I will forgive their iniquity, and their sin will remember no more.

Is vitally important to understand that the Jeremiah promise has already been fulfilled in the new covenant that Jesus Christ left us in Hebrews chapter 8:1,6. And in Romans chapter 11:23, 27 when all of Israel is finally grafted if they do not continue in unbelief, it will then be materialized in their lives. And this particular deliverer has already come from Zion and his name is Jesus Christ. That is why it is so vitally important to reach the beautiful Jewish people around the world for their deliverer have already come from Zion.

In second Corinthians chapter 3:3 being manifested that you are a letter of Christ, cared for by us, written not

with ink, but with the Spirit of the living God, not on tablets of stone, but on tablets of human hearts.

In first John chapter 2:27 And for you, the anointing which you received from him abides in you, and you have no need for anyone to teach you; but as his anointing teaches you about all things, and is true and it's not a lie, and just that it has taught you, you abide in him.

As born again believers we have a new life, the ZOE kind of life, the spirit of Almighty God lives within us, we have become a written letter of Christ not written with natural ink, by the spirit of the living God, and it was not written on hard tablets, but it was written on our human hearts, just as it will be in the hearts of the beautiful Jewish people when they make Jesus Christ their Savior and Lord.

Now in John 2: 27 every born-again believer that has received the baptism in the Holy Spirit, has a particular anointing that abides with us and in us forever, and we have no need for anybody to teach us the word of God, but it is his anointing that does the teaching, and that anointing is true and is not a lie, and as he has taught us we will abide in him.

In the gospel of John chapter 6:45 "It is written in the prophets, and they shall all be taught of God,' everyone who has heard and learn from the father, comes to me.

In the first letter of John chapter 2:20, 23 But you have an anointing from the holy one, and you all know.

Verse 21, I have not written to you because you do not know the truth.

Verse 22, who is the liar but the one who denies that Jesus is the Christ? This is the antichrist, the one who denies the father and the son.

Verse 23 whoever denies the son does not have a father; the one who confesses the son has the father also.

See you see my brothers and my sisters those of you who are reading this book, through the Lordship of Jesus Christ, we have accepted the last covenant that God has already made with humanity, there is no other covenant coming after this one for neither Jewish nor Gentiles, but the rapture, the next major event is the catching away of the Saints, and because we have made Jesus Christ our Lord and Savior, this holy Scripture has been written in our hearts by the power and the anointing of the Holy Spirit, and we don't need any human beings to teach us but the Holy Spirit that lives and abides with us forever.

And even Jesus said in the gospel of John 6:45 but it was written by the prophets, so he himself even talked about Jeremiah the prophet, which we would all be taught by God himself through the anointing of the Holy Spirit, and they that had heard and learned from the father would come to Jesus.

So in Hebrews chapter 10:14, 22 For by one offering he has perfected for all time those who are sanctified.

Verse 15, and the Holy Spirit also bears witness to us; for after saying,

Verse 16, "this is the covenant that I will make with them after those days says the Lord: I will put my laws upon their heart, and upon their mind I will write them," he then says,

Verse 17, "And their sins and their lawless deeds I will remember no more."

Verse 18, now where there is forgiveness of these things, there is no longer any offering for sin.

Verse 19, Since therefore, brethren, we have confidence to enter the holy place by the blood of Jesus,

Verse 20, by a new and living way which he inaugurated for us through the veil, that is, his flesh,

Verse 21, and since we have a great priest over the house of God,

Verse 22, let us draw near with a sincere heart in full assurance of faith, having our hearts sprinkled clean from an evil conscience and our bodies washed with pure water.

Verse 23, Let us hold fast the confession of our hope without wavering, for he who promised is faithful:

Everyone that has believed in the Lordship of Jesus Christ has confidence to enter into the holy of holies by the blood of Jesus Christ.

Because he has already opened up a new and living way by inaugurating through his flesh the removal of the veil, and therefore we have access into the throne room of Almighty God.

Thank God, we have, a new covenant, New Testament:

GOD SAYS, THAT I HAVE, (A NEW CONFIDENCE)

In the first letter of John chapter 5:14,15 And this is the confidence which we have before him, that, if we ask anything according to his will, he hears us.

Verse 15, And if we know that he hears us in whatever we ask, we know that we have the requests which we have asked from him.

This is why it's so important to take this book and read it back and forth because what you are reading it is not something that God is going to do for your life, but what God has already done through Jesus Christ in our behalf, so that, gives us confidence when we ask something according to his word, according to his will, according to his testament, according to what he has already promised belongs to us, we are doing absolutely nothing different than believing his inheritance for us his children, under this new covenant.

In the letter of James chapter 5:14, 15 is anyone among you sick? Let them call the elders of the church, and let them pray over him, anointing him with oil in the name of the Lord;

Verse 15, and the prayer offered in faith will restore the one who is sick, and the Lord will raise him up, and if he has committed sins, they will be forgiven him.

We have the right to call the elders of the church when we are sick, they can come and visit us and anoint us with oil in the name of the Lord.

And if the Preacher or elder of this church knows how to pray the prayer of faith, we have the right in Jesus name to be healed, for by his stripes we were healed.

We have a new Hope, we have a new expectancy, we have through Christ the right to be made whole, thank God for his precious blood on the cross.

In first John chapter 3:7,8 Little children, let no one deceive you; the one who practices righteousness is righteous, just as he is righteous;

Verse eight, the one who practices sin is of the devil; for the devil has sinned from the beginning. The son of God appeared for this purpose, that he might destroy the works of the devil.

For this reason we have the power, the privilege to practice righteousness, because our Lord and Savior who lives in us is righteous, we Christians no longer live to commit sin, or live practicing sin, because it is for this reason that Jesus Christ came, that he might destroy the works of the devil, that had us blinded and enslaved, thank God his precious blood cleansed and broke every power of the enemy in our lives, and gave us a new life.

GOD SAYS, THAT I HAVE, (POWER OVER THE DEVIL AND HIS DEMONS)

And in Luke's gospel chapter 10:19 "behold, I have given you authority to tread upon serpents and scorpions, and over all the power of the enemy, and nothing shall injure you.

In other translation it says Behold, I give unto you power to tread on serpents and scorpions, and over all the power of the enemy: and nothing shall by any means hurt you.

Whether you call it authority or you call it power, in the name of Jesus we have the authority, and we have the power to tread upon serpents and scorpions and upon all the power of the enemy, and nothing shall by any means hurt us, hallelujah.

In this new King James version, the gospel of Mark chapter 16:15,18 and he said unto them, go ye into all the world, and preach the gospel to every creature.

Verse 16, He that believeth and is baptized shall be saved; but he that believeth not shall damned.

Verse 17, And these signs shall follow them that believe; in my name shall they cast out devils; they shall speak with new tongues;

Verse 18, They shall take up serpents; and if they drink any deadly thing, it shall not hurt them; they shall lay hands on the sick, and they shall recover.

We have power, we have the delegated authority cast out demons and Devils, to lay hands on the sick and they shall recover and that settles it.

God is not dead he is alive and well, and Jesus Christ of Nazareth is our heavenly lawyer at the right hand of God the father interceding for us day and night that we might develop a godly and biblical identity, believing all of his promises, receiving all of his delegated authorities, believing what is our right and privileges in Christ, and standing upon the God given power through the baptism of the Holy Spirit.

GOD SAYS, THAT I HAVE, (A LAWYER, AN ADVOCATE, WITH GOD)

In the first letter of John chapter 2:1,2 My little children, I am writing these things to you that you may not sin, and if anyone sins, we have an advocate with the father, Jesus Christ the righteous.

Verse two, and he himself is the propitiation for our sins; and not for ours only, but also for those of the whole world.

In the epistle to the Hebrews chapter 7:19, 25 (for the law made nothing perfect), and on the other hand there is a bringing in of a better hope, through which we draw near to God.

Verse 20, Inasmuch as it was not without oath

Verse 21, (for they indeed became priests without an oath, but he with an oath through the one who said to him, "The Lord has sworn And I will not change his mind, 'Thou art a priest forever'");

Verse 22, so much the more also Jesus has become the guarantee of a better covenant.

Verse 23, In the former priests, on the one hand, existed in greater numbers, because they were prevented by death from continuing,

Verse 24, but he, on the other hand, because he abides forever, holds his priesthood permanently.

Verse 25, Hence, also, He is able to save forever those who draw near to God through him, since he always lives to make intercession for them.

As you may very well have read according to the law the priests could not continue ministering in the holy of holies because of death, but because Jesus Christ lives forever and holds his priesthood permanently, we can draw near to God Almighty which is our heavenly father thanks to the shed blood of Jesus Christ on the cross.

Every born-again believer around the world has a high priest that lives forever interceding at the right hand of the father forever, since he always lives to make intercession for us, he is better than an earthly lawyer, for any situation, we have a heavenly lawyer, who has never lost the case, that in spite of everything we have gone through, he always lives to make intercession for us. Hallelujah.

As I write these words I find it so comforting that we are not left alone in this world, that the comforter the Holy Spirit lives within us, and that we can talk to God in the name of Jesus and know that our spirit bears witness with his spirit that we are his children, and that because we have an advocate at the right hand of the father, we know that in spite of the fact that sometimes we don't get all the answers when we want them, and at the time and in the manner of which we prayed, we know that our heavenly lawyer who is seated at the right hand of the father will see to it that he gets our petition, and that these petitions get answered as soon as possible.

GOD SAYS, THAT I CAN, (DO ALL THINGS IN CHRIST)

In Philippians chapter 4:12, 13 I know how to get along with humble means, and I also know how to live in prosperity; in any and every circumstance I have learned the secret of being filled and going hungry, both of having abundance and suffering need.

Verse 13, I can do all things through him who strengthens me.

Contrary to a lot of teachings around the world, I have always heard that Philippians 4:13 it was about doing anything in the natural, or doing anything that had to do with business, or anything that has to do with exercise, and anything else that had to do with what I could, or could not do. Because this is the way it was explained to me, but the truth of the matter is, when almost everything else I ever did failed, and found myself in the gutter, because for some reason a lot of people don't think that one day they'll be in the Valley, that's when I understood that it had to do with getting along with a lot, as well as getting along with almost nothing.

Here we see the apostle Paul saying that he is able to get along with humble means, and that he also knows how to live in prosperity, and that in any circumstance he found himself in, he had learned the secret of being filled or going hungry, and also of both having abundance or suffering need, and that is when he says on verse 13 a powerful word that we have heard quoted around the world, I can do all things through Jesus Christ who strengthens me.

The important thing in life is whether you're up, or down, whether you have money, or have needs, whether you're on the mountaintop, or in the Valley, whether you are married, or you are divorced, whether you are sick, or whether you're healthy, whether you have a healthy outlook about yourself, or a poor old me syndrome, our heavenly father will never leave us nor forsake us, and if we are in the Valley, we can go no lower, he will raise us up to the mountaintop, and we will reap in do season if we do not faint.

GOD SAYS, THAT I CAN, (LIVE WORRY FREE)

In Romans chapter 8:32, 39 He who did not spare his own son, but delivered him up for us all, how will he not also with him freely give us all things?

Verse 33, Who will bring a charge against God's elect? God is the one who justifies.

Verse 34, who is the one who condemns? Christ Jesus is he who died, yes, rather who was raised, who is at the right hand of God, who also intercedes for us.

Verse 35, Who shall separate us from the love of Christ? Shall tribulation, or distress, or persecution, or famine, or nakedness, or peril, or sword?

Verse 36, Just as it is written, "For thy sake we are being put to death all day long; We were considered as sheep to be slaughtered."

Verse 37 But in all these things we overwhelmingly conquer through him who loved us.

Verse 38, For I am convinced that neither death, nor life, nor angels, nor principalities, nor things present, nor things to come, nor powers,

Verse 39, nor height, nor depth, nor any other created thing, shall be able to separate us from the love of God, which is in Christ Jesus our Lord.

He who did not spare his own son, but he delivered him up for us all, how will he not also with him, freely give us all things, and that means whatever we need, hallelujah.

We are God's elect, and no one can bring a charge against us, it is only God who justifies the sinner through the shed blood of his son Jesus, who was dead, and is now raised, and is seated at the right hand of the father interceding for us.

In spite of the fact that we go through ups and downs, situation's with money and situations without money, valleys, and mountaintops, who shall separate us from the love of Christ who lives within our hearts? Shall tribulation, distress, persecution, or famine, or nakedness, or peril, or sword?

Sometimes we feel that we are sheep taken to be slaughtered, here we see the apostle Paul say for thy sake we are being put to death all day long. Sometimes we feel just like the apostle Paul himself as we go through our trials and tribulations.

In the King James Version of the Bible Romans chapter 8:37 Nay, in all these things we are more than conquerors through him that loved us.

Jesus Christ conquered all of these trials and tribulations that all of us have gone through, that's why he says in all of these things we are more than conquerors through him that loved us.

So we should be persuaded because of everything we have been reading so far, God in Christ, Jesus in us makes us more than conquerors, that is why neither death, nor life, neither angels, or principalities, nor things that are present, nor things that will come, nor powers, nor height or depth, nor any other created thing can separate us from the love of God which is in Christ Jesus who lives within us.

GOD SAYS, THAT I CAN, (RECEIVE ANSWERS TO MY PRAYERS)

In first John chapter 5:15 And if we know that he hears us in whatever we ask, we know that we have the requests which we have asked from him.

In the gospel of John chapter 14:13, 14 "And whatever you ask in my name, that will I do, that the father may be glorified in the son.

Verse 14, "If you ask me anything in my name, I will do it.

And in the gospel of John 15:7 "If you abide in me, and my words abide in you, ask whatever you wish, and it shall be done for you.

Here we see the son of God saying that we should pray and ask the father in the name of Jesus and he is guaranteeing that we will have what so ever we ask, and then he says in verse seven that if we abide in his words, and his words are part of our everyday living, that we should ask whatever we wish, and it shall be done for us.

And on verse 11 he says these things I have spoken to you, that my joy may be in you, and that your joy may be made full.

God wants us all happy, and unless our prayers are answered we will not be happy, so he said to ask the father in the name of Jesus, and he himself guaranteed that he would get it done. Unless our prayers are been heard, and the answers start coming our way, a) we will not be happy, and b) we will not be receiving the response to our prayers.

GOD SAYS, THAT I CAN,
(FIGHT THE GOOD FIGHT OF FAITH)

In the first letter of Paul to Timothy chapter 6:11, 12 But free from these things, you men of God; and pursue righteousness, godliness, faith, love, perseverance and gentleness.

Verse 12, Fight the good fight of faith; take hold of eternal life to which you were called, and you made the good confession in the presence of many witnesses.

The Bible says that we have a faith fight, not a devil fight, but a faith fight, he called us man of God, and to pursue righteousness, godliness, faith, love, perseverance and gentleness, which will require faith, for all of these things have already being put inside of us, through the person of the Lord Jesus Christ, that is why he wants us to fight the good fight of faith, because it's the enemy trying to take away what God has already put inside of us, and that is the spirit of Christ, who bears witness with our spirit that we are sons of God.

And in second Timothy 4:5,7 But you, be sober in all things, endure hardship, do the work of an evangelist, fulfill your ministry.

Verse six, For I am already being poured out as a drink offering, and the time of my departure has come.

Verse seven, I have fought the good fight, I have finished the course, I have kept the faith;

Here we see the apostle Paul saying to Timothy to be sober in all things and to endure hardship, and to do the work of an evangelist, thereby fulfilling his ministry.

And he said the magic words his departure for heaven had already come, and that he had fought the good fight of faith, and that he had finished the course, and that he had kept the faith.

Every attack of the enemy, every onslaught of fiery darts against us, every negative thought, every worry, every concern, every fear that we will all go through, he said that we could overcome it by faith, because we have the shield of faith, and the sword of the spirit, which is the word of God, to speak with our mouth and to believe we our hearts what doth sayeth God.

In Romans 12, 3 for I say, through the grace given unto me, to every man that is among you, not to think of himself more highly than he ought to think; but to think soberly, according as God has dealt to every man the measure of faith.

But to think soberly according as God has dealt to every man the measure of faith.

In Romans 10:17 So then faith cometh by hearing, and hearing by the word of God.

Every Christian in the world has a measure of faith deposited within us, and that measure of faith can grow, and it can also go away, depending on whether we are hearing the word of God, or reading the word of God, but faith can come, and faith can leave, that is why it's so important for us to go to church and listen to the word of God being preached, and to read the word of God daily, so that faith can come by hearing, and hearing by the word of God.

As the apostle Paul said that we needed to fight the good fight of faith, he was encouraging us to realize that all we have is a faith fight, which is why he said that we wrestle not against flesh and blood, but against principalities, against powers, and against rulers of this Dark Age, and spiritual wickedness in high places. Not human beings, but it's the enemy whispering in our minds, that we are worthless, that we will never amount to anything, we will never reach any goals in our lives, and that we are going under, and that will never have any success in any area of our lives, it is the enemy attacking us, not human beings, that is why it's so important to analyze our minds on a daily basis of what we're thinking about, for it is there that we have our greatest battles.

In Colossians chapter 2:15 And having spoiled principalities and powers, he made a show of them openly, triumphing over them in it.

Our elder brother triumphed over them, principalities, and powers, and rulers of this dark age on the cross, so that you and I could be free, so that you and I could be handed over the victory, so that you and I could be handed the New Testament, stipulating that the victory is ours, Jesus came to destroy the works of the devil and he did it, the devil has no right, the devil has no power over our lives anymore, neither ours nor our children, that's why the apostle Paul said to fight the good fight of faith, why was it a good fight of faith, because the victory has already been won and handed over to us.

GOD SAYS, THAT I CAN, (OVERCOME THE WORLD)

In the first epistle of John chapter 5:4, 5 Whatsoever is born of God overcomes the world: and this is the victory that overcomes the world, even our faith.

Verse five, Who is he that overcomes the world, but he that believe that Jesus is the son of God?

Every born-again believer has been born of God, with the God kind of life in us, with the seed of God in us, with the righteousness of God in us, with the nature of God in us, with the divine nature in us, with eternal life in us, with the power of God in us to thread over serpents and scorpions, and over all the power of the enemy, that is why he says that with all of that we can overcome the world, through the measure of faith that was deposited within us, through faith in the Lordship of Jesus Christ.

There is no lust of the eyes, there is no lust of the flesh, there is no pride of life, in that the enemy can throw against us, for we have been born of God and given the power to overcome the world, hallelujah.

GOD SAYS, THAT I CAN, (WALK IN THE SPIRIT)

In the epistle of Paul to the Galatians chapter 5: 16, 17 But I say, walk by the spirit, and you will not carry out the desire of the flesh.

Verse 17, For the flesh sets its desire against the spirit, and the Spirit against the flesh; for these are in opposition to one another, that you may not do the things that you please.

Verse 18, But if you are led by the spirit, you are not under the law.

When Paul says that we can walk in the spirit, that means we are no longer victims to our flesh, we are no longer slaves to our thought life, we are no longer slaves to our flesh, we are no longer slaves to the fiery darts of the enemy, and we are no longer slaves at all.

For the apostle Paul knew that the greatest warfare that the Christian has, is the spirit of God within us wanting to do the will of God, and the flesh where it is that we live in warring against our spirit, and this is the greatest problem that every Christian has.

For every true born-again believer wants to do the will of God, they want to serve God day and night, they want to go to church at all times, it's within our hearts.

And only those that are led by the spirit, the fruit of the spirit, are not under the law.

And in Galatians 5:19, 25 Now the deeds of the flesh are evident, which are: immorality, impurity, sensuality,

Verse 20, idolatry, sorcery, enmities, strife, jealousy, outbursts of anger, disputes, dissension, factions,

Verse 21, envying, drunkenness, carousing, and things like these, of which I forewarn you as I have forewarn you to those who practice such things shall not inherit the kingdom of God.

Verse 22, but the fruit of the spirit is love, joy, peace, patience, kindness, goodness, faithfulness,

Verse 23, gentleness, self-control; against such things there is no law.

Verse 24, Of those who belong to Christ Jesus have crucified the flesh with its passions and desires.

Verse 25, If we live by the spirit, let us also walk by the spirit.

And this is the victory for all of us on verse 24, of those who belong to Christ Jesus have crucified the flesh with its passions and desires.

So if we live by the spirit which means treat others with love, live a joyful life, live a peaceful life, and to exercise patience, kindness, goodness, and faithfulness, gentleness and self-control, against these things there is no law, for these are the fruit of the spirit and not of human effort, we will no longer fulfill the lust of the flesh, it is an act of our will.

GOD SAYS, THAT I CAN, (FORGIVE OTHERS)

In the gospel of Matthew's chapter 6:14, 15 "For if you forgive men for their transgressions, your heavenly father will also forgive you.

Verse 15, "But if you do not forgive men, then your father will not forgive your transgressions.

In the gospel of Mark chapter 11:25, 26 "And whenever you stand praying, forgive, if you have anything against anyone; so that your father also who is in heaven may forgive you your transgressions.

Verses 26, "But if you do not forgive, neither will your father who is in heaven forgive your transgressions."

Thank God that we can forgive people, thank God that we can bring people to God in prayer, so that God can be the judge of their lives and not us, thank God we no longer have to carry the burden, and the rejection, if we re-buke a brother or a sister who has done us wrong, thank God we can just bring them to him and he takes care of it all, we no longer have to carry the grudge against anybody, we just hand them over to God.

But you may say pastor this is very tough to do, when God says we can do it, there's no question about it, if he said it we have to believe it and that settles it, now in the natural it may seem impossible, but in Christ we can do all things.

GOD SAYS, THAT I CAN,
(CAST ALL MY CARES UPON HIM)

In first Peter chapter 5:7 casting all your anxiety, cares, upon him, because he cares for you.

And the Bible says that we can cast all of our cares upon him because he cares for us, the word cares means, all anxiety, all worries, all Greif, all consequences of what others have done against us, or what we have done against them.

Now obvious I had to go to the Webster dictionary to find out some of these words, so I looked up the first word anxiety, 1) disturbance of mind regarding some uncertain event, 2) strained or solicitous desire, as for some object or purpose.

Synonyms, 1) anguish, 2) apprehension, 3) care, 4) concern, 5) disturbance, 6) dread, 7) fear, 8) Fretfulness, 9) Fretting, 10) Misgiving, 11) perplexity, 12) trouble, 13) worry.

Anxiety refers to some future event, always suggesting hopeful possibility, and thus deferring from apprehension, fear, dread, for boarding, error, all of which may be quite despairing. Worry is a prettier, restless, and manifests anxiety.

Anxiety may be quiet and silent; Worry is communicated to all around. Solitude is a milder anxiety. Fretting or fretfulness is a weak complaining without thought of accomplishing or changing anything, but merely as a relief to one's own disquiet.

Perplexity often involves anxiety, but may be quite free from it.

One feels anxiety for a friend's return; anxiety about, for, in regards to, or concerning the future.

Antonyms: 1) apathy, 2) assurance, 3) calmness, 4) carelessness, 5) confidence, 6) peace, 7) lightheadedness, 8) nonchalance, 9) satisfaction, 10) tranquility.

Now through prayer if we do a careful examination on our emotions, on our thought life, on our nerves, on our lack of sleep at night and ask God in Jesus name to reveal to us what is causing us to feel any one of these previously mentioned anxieties, he will reveal it to us thereby allowing us to bring it to God in prayer and casting it upon him, casting upon him means asking him to take it away, asking him to deliver you from it, asking him to take the load from you, and believing by faith that when you get up from prayer, that you have released the load, that you have asked to take it away from you, or that he has taken it away from you, and by faith go back to sleeping, or Get up and do your everyday household chores. When you ask you must believe that you receive and you shall have Mark 11:24.

Thank God that we can communicate with our heavenly father in the name of the Lord Jesus Christ of Nazareth, and know that he hears our prayers, and know that he can take away the load, and we can cast all of our cares upon him, and know that he will take away the pain, and know that he can, and will take away the rejection, it's so good to know that everyone is imperfect, and when every career has fails, when every family member has failed to be there for us, God is there, and he hears our prayers, and he knows when our bodies, our minds, and our emotions cannot go on any longer, we can come to him with our heads bowed and all of our worries and cast them on him.

Thank God that when all fails, our heavenly father, our heavenly daddy, is there and is listening to our humble cry, I love you Lord with all my heart.

Our heavenly father does really cares for us.

GOD SAYS, THAT I CAN, (RENEW MY MIND, WITH THE WORD)

In the epistle of Paul to the Romans chapter 12:1,2 I urge you therefore, brethren, by the mercies of God, to present your bodies a living and holy sacrifice, acceptable to God, which is your spiritual service of worship.

Verse two, and do not be conformed to this world, but be transformed by the renewing of your mind, that you may prove what the will of God is, that which is good and acceptable and perfect.

Here God is telling us to do two major things, which he knows that we can do.

1) To present our bodies a living sacrifice.
2) Holy and acceptable to God.
3) Which is our spiritual service of worship.
4) And do not be conformed to this world.
5) But be transformed by the renewing of your mind.
6) So that we may prove what the good, perfect, and acceptable will of God is.

In order to renew our minds, we must have a Bible, we must read the Bible, and we must study the Bible, and that in itself is a living sacrifice holy and acceptable to God.

If we are saved, if we are spirit filled, and our minds are clouded, our minds are confused, we are heirs of all these blessings but it will not help us in any way shape or form, we must renew our thinking, our minds is like an airport where the enemy constantly lands, words that are abominable to God and contrary to the word of God, that is why the apostle Paul said, I urge you therefore brethren, he understood the importance of having an identity based on what God says and not necessarily on the negative thought life about ourselves that we constantly have, not because were bad people but because the enemy attacks us there.

No Christian has any business having a clouded mind or be led by his flesh, this is exactly what Jesus Christ came to do, to crucify our flesh, to clear up our minds, and to give us the wisdom from heaven that we so desperately needed, so that we could be spirit ruled, and not carnally minded.

God says that we can renew our mind, and it is to our benefit so that we may prove what is the good, the perfect, and acceptable will of God.

God wants us to be transformed in the image and likeness of his son Jesus our Savior and our Lord, that is the transformation that he wants us to have, and we are developing it.

GOD SAYS, THAT I CAN, (KNOW HIS WISDOM)

In the book of Proverbs chapter 3:13, 18 How blessed is the man who finds wisdom, and the man who gains understanding.

Verse 14, For its profit is better than the profit of silver, and its gain than fine gold.

Verse 15, She is more precious than jewels; and nothing you desire compares with her.

Verse 16, Long life is in her right hand; in her left hand riches and honor.

Verses 17, her ways are pleasant ways, and all her paths are peace.

Verse 18, She is a tree of life to those who take hold of her, and happy are all who hold her fast.

In the book of Proverbs chapter 4:5, 7 Acquire wisdom! Acquire understanding!

Do not forget, nor turn away from the words of my mouth.

Verse six, "Do not forsake her, and she will guard you; Love her, and she will watch over you.

Verse seven, "The beginning of wisdom is: Acquire wisdom; And with all your acquiring, get understanding.

We have no excuse God says we can get wisdom, and understanding and both of these words will do something in our lives, we can find it, and we can gain it, no excuses.

The original intent of this book is for us to get the identity that God has already purchased for us through Jesus Christ on the cross, claim our rights and privileges, and act upon our God-given power over the enemy, over our bodies, and over our thought life, God wants us to be prosperous in every area of our lives, that's why he says that we need wisdom and understanding, for they are better profit then silver and gold.

Wisdom and understanding are more precious than all the Jules of this world, and nothing that we would desire compares with her.

Long life is in her right hand, and in her left hand riches, and honor, her ways are pleasant ways, and her paths are peace, and all of us who take hold of her she is like a tree of life, and all of us will be happy who hold her fast in our hearts.

Here we see our heavenly father encouraging us to never forsake her, and she will guard us, and as we love her she will watch over us.

These are powerful words, isn't this supernatural, that God, the creator of the heavens and the earth used his pencil called Salomon to write such beautiful wisdom, who intricately and supernaturally breathed through his pencil and wrote such a masterpiece.

GOD SAYS, THAT I CAN, (FIND, KNOW, AND DO HIS WILL)

One very important Man said, to find the will of God, is our greatest discovery.

To know the will of God is our greatest knowledge.

To do the will of God is our greatest achievement.

In order to find, to know, and to do the will of God, we must look to Jesus Christ who is the Arthur and finisher of our faith.

In the gospel of Mark chapter 3: 35 "For whoever does the will of God, he is my brother and my sister and my mother."

And in the gospel of John chapter 4:34 Jesus said to them, "My food is to do the will of him who sent me, and to accomplish his work.

And in the same gospel of John chapter 5:30 "I can do nothing on my own initiative. As I hear, I judge; and my judgment is just, because I do not seek my own will, but the will of him who sent me.

And in John chapter 6:39, 40 "And this is the will of him who sent me, that of all that he has given me I lose nothing, but raise it up on the last day.

Verse 40, "For this is the will of my father that everyone who beholds the son and believes in him, may have an eternal life; and I myself will raise him up on the last day."

And finally in the book of acts chapter 13:21, 22 "And then they asked for a king, and God gave them Saul the son of Kish, a man of the tribe of Benjamin, for 40 years.

Verse 22, "And after he had removed him, he raised up David to be their king, concerning whom he also testified and said, I have found David the son of Jesse, a man after my heart, who will do all my will.

It is definitely obvious that God is looking for a man who will do his will, and Jesus Christ himself said whoever does the will of my father, he is my brother and my sister and my mother, and he also said that his food was to do the will of him who sent him, and that he needed to accomplish his work which as you very well may now, was to lay down his life as a sacrificed Lamb, a sacrificial Lamb, between a holy God and a sinful creature, so that his precious blood could wash away all our sin, and that is the good news.

Jesus Christ said it himself, everything he ever heard from the father he spoke, and it was what he did.

He also said that the will of the father is that every human being they came to him for salvation, and forgiveness of sin, he will not lose, but he would raise them up on the last day.

In Jesus also said that whoever would believe in him as their Savior and Lord, we would have eternal life, and at the last day he would raise us up.

The greatest disaster, for the life of a human being, is to reach his ripe old age, and never find, and never know, and never do, the will of God, the greatest and the most important thing in my own personal life that I would dread tremendously, is to get old and depart to heaven, and never hear the words of Jesus come in my good and faithful servant, enter into your rest, but to hear him say Matthew's chapter 7:23 And then I will declare to them, I never knew you; depart from me, you who practice lawlessness, in other translation it says you worker of iniquity, for I never knew you. And believe you me that in that day a lot of people will say Matthew 7:22 Many will say to me in that they, Lord, Lord, did we not prophesy in your name, and in your name cast out demons, and in your name perform many miracles?'

Verse 23 I never knew you depart for me you worker of iniquity.

Now the will of God for Jesus was to seek and to save that which was lost, to never lose any believer to the devil and at the last days to raise them up.

Now the will of God for David who was a man after God's own heart, was to rule all of Israel, to govern and fulfill God's covenant with him, and to carry out God's calling on his life, and to give him an heir of the throne of Israel, which was Solomon.

The word Bible, the word old, and new testament, the word covenant, and the word will of God, are synonymous with God's desire, which was hand written with his pencils(human beings) in his holy letter of love towards us.

In Hebrews chapter 9:14, 17 How much more shall the blood of Christ, who through the eternal Spirit offered himself without spot to God, purge your conscience from dead works to serve the living God?

Versus 15, And for this cause he is the mediator of a new testament, that by means of death, for the redemption of the transgressions that were under the first testament, they which are called may receive the promise of eternal inheritance.

Verse 16 For where a testament is, there must also of necessity be the death of the testator.

Verse 17, For a testament is of force after men are dead: otherwise it is of no strength at all while the testator lives.

Now let's realize how the blood of Jesus Christ shed on the cross, purge our conscience from dead works, to serve the living God. Please notice God's ultimate goal is to serve him.

So the purging of our conscience from dead works was necessary.

Now we know that our testator died, was buried, and rose triumphantly over death hell and the grave and is seated at the right hand of the father.

And we know that he came to seek and to save that which was lost.

And that which was lost was you and I reading this book, and thanks to his holy blood we have been cleansed and washed and saved.

And he went to heaven and sat at the right hand of the father and became our heavenly lawyer, for he ever lived to make intercession for us.

And this testator lived, died, was buried, was raised, and is alive forever more.

This new testator Jesus Christ left us a new testament, with every single message, with every single principle, with every single priority and values, and the good news for human beings, in every area of their lives, and what you and I will ever need is already written.

In this precious New Testament, we find the will of God, because Jesus came to fulfill it, and when you and I read the New Testament we are reading God's will, and that settles it.

GOD'S WILL, (GODLY IDENTITY, NEW CHRISTIAN BEHAVIOR)

I Can Find, Know, And do, God's Will:

In first Thessalonians chapter 4:1, 12 Furthermore then we beseech you, brethren, and exhort you by the Lord Jesus, that as ye have received of us how ye ought to walk and to please God, so you would abound more and more.

Verse two, For ye know what commandments we gave you by the Lord Jesus.

Verse three, For this is the will of God, even your sanctification, that you should abstain from fornication:

Verse four, That every one of you should know how to possess his vessel in sanctification and honor.

Verse five, Not in the lusts of concupiscence, even as the Gentiles which know not God:

Verse six, That no man go beyond and defraud his brother in any matter: because that the Lord is the avenger of all such, as we also have forewarned you and testified.

Verse seven, For God has not called us unto uncleanness, but unto holiness.

Verse eight, He therefore that despiseth, despiseth not man, but God, who has also given unto us his Holy Spirit.

Verse nine, But as touching brotherly love you need not that I write unto you: for ye yourselves are taught of God to love one another.

Verse 10 And indeed you do it toward all the brethren which are all in Macedonia: but we beseech you, brethren, that you increase more and more:

Verse 11, And that you study to be quiet, and to do your own business, and to work with your own hands, as we commanded you.

Verse 12, That ye may walk honestly toward them that are without, and that you may have lack of nothing.

Now as we read God's will, which is God's word, on these paragraphs we see the apostle Paul beseeching the Thessalonians and exhorting them of the message they had already received from him, which was in the manner they should have conducted themselves in order to please God Almighty, so that they would abound more and more in that conduct.

He was telling them that he had already given them by the Lord Jesus Christ the commandment.

And in verse three, For this is the will of God, the apostle Paul is giving us God's will in order for us to know how we are conduct ourselves, in 18 different topics.

1) How we ought to walk, 2) We should abound more and more, 3) It is a commandment, 4) It is the will of God, 5) To live a life of sanctification, 6) To abstain from fornication, 7) That we should know how to obtain our vessel(body), 8) Not in lusts as Gentiles that don't know God, 9) Not to defraud our brothers, 10) God will protect those people we defraud, 11) God did not call us to uncleanness, 12) If we despise this teaching, we are despising God,

13) God has given us his Holy Spirit, 14) God by his Holy Spirit will teach us about love, 15) God wants us to work with our hands, 16) God wants us to live a quiet life, 17) God wants us to be honest in dealing with the people that don't have any, 18) and ultimately all of this conduct will lead us to not lacking anything, which is our gain.

All these 18 topics we have just read in first Thessalonians there is no excuse for us not to do the will of God, because it is a commandment, and we are the beneficiary of a new conduct in Christ.

In first Thessalonians chapter 5:16, 23 Rejoice evermore.

Verse 17, Pray without ceasing.

Verses 18, in everything give thanks: for this is the will of God in Christ Jesus concerning you.

Verse 19, Quench not the spirit.

Verse 20, Despise not prophesying's,

Verse 21, Prove all things; hold fast that which is good.

Verse 22, Abstain from all appearance of evil.

Verse 23, And the very God of peace sanctify you wholly; and I pray God your whole spirit and soul and body be preserved blameless unto the coming of our Lord Jesus Christ.

1) Here the apostle Paul is telling us to rejoice in whatever situation we find ourselves in.

2) He wants us to pray without ceasing.

3) Notice what he said, In everything, not For everything, give thanks, For this is the will of God concerning us.

4) He does not want us to quench the Holy Spirit that lives in us, how do we quench the Holy Spirit? 1) by lying, 2) by cheating, 3) by defrauding our brothers, 4) by watching pornography, 5) by living a life of uncleanness, and fornicating, 6) by idolatry, 7) by doing our will, 8) by not reading the word, 9) by not going to church, 10) by not supporting the work of God, 11) by rejecting our brothers, 12) by not forgiving people, 13) by not walking in love, 14) by not surrendering to God's word, 15) by not walking in faith.

5) Despise not the prophecies that are being given to you, if they do come from God.

6) Prove everything that is being said to you, and hold to that which is true.

7) For all of us to abstain from any evil appearance.

8) And finally notice that we are a spirit, possessing a soul, and living inside our body, being preserved blameless to the coming of our Lord.

On these other new eight revelations we have now found, we now know, and we can now do, the will of our heavenly father, no questions asked.

Now we can go around the world telling people that we have found, and that we know, and from now on we will do the will of our heavenly father on these 26 topics, and that settles it.

After reading this book we will never ever again questioned what the will of God is for our lives, it is a Christ like conduct, to be changed in the image and likeness of Christ.

GOD'S WILL, HIS CHURCH, THE CORPORATE BODY OF CHRIST, MY POSITION?

Now in the body of Christ we have many members, 1) We have the sheep, 2) We have the ushers, 3) We have the deacons, 4) We have the elders, 5) We have The apostles, 6) We have the prophets, 7) We have the evangelists, 8) We have the pastors, 9) We have the teachers, And these are the fivefold ministry gifts. This is found in Ephesians chapter 4:11.

> **In first Corinthians chapter 12:28, 29 And God has appointed in the church, first apostles, second prophets, third teachers, then miracles, then gifts of healings, helps, administration, various kinds of tongues.**
>
> **Verse 29, All are not apostles, are they? All are not prophets, are they? All are not teachers, are they? All are not workers of miracles, are they?**
>
> **Verse 30, All do not have gifts of healing, do they? All do not speak with tongues, do they? All do not interpret, do they?**
>
> **Verse 31 But earnestly desire the greater gifts. And I show you a still more excellent way.**

Now in finding the will of God for our lives, we need to ask God in Jesus name where do we fit in one of those gifts that God himself set in the church, that we could be fruitful and help the growth of the local church, we are not to be parasites, we are not to go by blaming churches, we are not to go by in life fault finding, we are not to criticize the members, the elders, and the different functions in the church, for this is not the will of God.

God himself will have to do the revealing, no human being can do that for us, it is our responsibility to pray without ceasing so that we may now God's perfect will for our lives in one of these positions within the local church.

Now the office of the Bishop, is a lot greater and higher than any other member in the body of Christ, and we are about to read the prerequisite for his office.

Now the word Bishop is EPISKOPOS, which means overseer found in the book of acts chapter 20:28 "Be on guard for yourselves and for all the flock, among which the Holy Spirit has made you overseers, to shepherd the church of God which he purchased with his own blood. Paul considers the elders of the church as overseers.

Now in order to be a Bishop we must develop the following prerequisites.

GOD'S WILL, (HIS PREREQUISITE FOR BISHOP, OVERSEER, ELDER)

In first Timothy chapter 3:1, 7 This is a true saying, if a man desire the office of a bishop, he desires a good work.

Verse two, A bishop then must be blameless, the husband of one wife, vigilant, sober, of good behavior, given to hospitality, apt to teach;

Verse three, Not given to wine, no striker, not greedy of filthy lucre; but patient, not a brawler, not covetousness;

Verse four, One that rules well his own house, having his children in subjection with all gravity;

Verse five, (For if a man know not how to rule his own house, how shall he take care of the church of God?)

Verse six, Not a novice, lest being lifted up with pride he fall into the condemnation of the devil.

Verse seven, Moreover he must have a good report of them which are without; lest he fall into reproach and the snare of the devil.

The prerequisite for any of the fivefold ministry gifts are very clear and evident in the first letter of Paul to Timothy chapter 3:1, 7.

There are 22 things that an elder, or a Bishop, one of the fivefold ministry gifts ministers has to learn to develop in his life before he can desire the office of a bishop.

1) A sincere and heart felt desire, 2) Must be blameless individual, 3) A husband of one wife, 4) A vigilant person, 5) A sober person, 6) A good behavior, 7) Given to hospitality, 8) Apt To teach, 9) Not given to wine, 10) Not a striker, 11) Not greedy of filthy lucre, 12) Must be patient, 13) Not a brawler, 14) Not a covetousness, 15) One that rules well his house, 16) Having obedient and subjected children, 17) Not a person that does not know how to rule his house, 18) If so how will he know how to rule the Church of God, 19) Not a Novice, 20) Not one that could be easily lifted up with pride, 21) One with a good report, 22) If not he will fall in the snare of the devil.

GOD'S WILL,
(HIS PREREQUISITE FOR A DEACON)

This is found in first Timothy chapter 3:8, 13 Deacons likewise must be man of dignity, not double tongue, or addicted to much wine or fond of sordid gain,

Verse nine, but holding to the mystery of the faith with a clear conscience.

Verse 10, let these also first be tested; then let them serve as beacons if they are beyond reproach.

Verse 11, Women must likewise be dignified, not malicious gossips, but temperate, faithful in all things.

Verse 12, Let deacons be husbands of only one wife, and good managers of their children and their own households.

Verse 13, For those who have served well as deacons obtain for themselves a high standing and great confidence in the faith that is in Christ Jesus.

GOD'S WILL,
(HIS PREREQUISITE, FOR A MINISTER)

This is found in first Timothy chapter 4:6, 7 If thou put the brethren in remembrance of these things, thou shalt be a good minister of Jesus Christ, nourished up in the words of faith and of good doctrine, whereunto thou has attained.

Verse seven, But refuse profane and old wives' fables, and exercise thyself rather unto godliness.

Now let's look at what he needs to put the brethren in remembrance of, in order to be a good minister of Jesus Christ, nourished in the words of faith and of a good doctrine.

In first Timothy chapter 3:16, and without controversy great is the mystery of godliness: God was manifested in the flesh, John 1:14, Justified in the Spirit Matthew 3:16, Seen of Angels Matthew 28:2, Preached unto the Gentiles Romans 10:19, 20.

Believed on in the world Colossians chapter 1:6, 23, Received up in glory. Luke 24:51

This is the message that a good solid minister ought to be teaching people, the apostle Paul calls it nourished in the words of faith and of a good doctrine, and also to warn of false prophets in the last days as we are about to read.

And this is found in first Timothy chapter 4:1, 5 Now the Spirit speaketh expressly, that in the latter times some shall depart from the faith, giving heed to seducing spirits, and doctrines of devils;

Verse two, Speaking lies in hypocrisy; having their conscience seared with a hot iron;

Verse three, forbidding marrying, and commanding to abstain from meats, which God hath created to be received with thanksgiving of them which believe and know the truth.

Verse four, For every creature of God is good, and nothing to be refused, if it be received with thanksgiving:

Verse five, For it is sanctified by the word of God and prayer.

This is the prerequisite for a good minister to have, a clear and precise message for the well-being of the flock of God, which is the church.

If we understand the story of the evangelical local church some are departing from the faith, giving heed to seducing spirits and doctrines of devils, and speaking all kinds of lies because their conscience are seared with a hot iron.

And some doctrines are telling their priests not to get married, and telling them to abstain from certain foods, which God had created to receive with thanksgiving of them who believe and know the truth.

Every single food that is presented before us if we pray over it, and ask God for his blessing upon it we are all able to eat it with no problem.

So I Can, find the will of God, Know the will of God, and Do the will of God.

GOD SAYS, THAT I CAN, (BE STRONG LIKE A SOLDIER AND AN ATHLETE)

In second Timothy chapter 2:1, 6 You therefore, my son, be strong in the grace that is in Christ Jesus.

Verse two, And the things which you have heard from me in the presence of many witnesses, these entrust to faithful men, who will be able to teach others also.

Verse three, Suffer hardship with me, as a good soldier of Christ Jesus.

Verse four, No soldier in active service and tangles himself in the affairs of everyday life, so that he may please the one who enlisted him as a soldier.

Verse five, And also if anyone competes as an athlete, he does not win the prize unless he competes according to the rules.

Verse six, the hard working farmer ought to be the first to receive his share of the crops.

Verse seven; consider what I say, for the Lord will give you understanding in everything.

When the Lord says to be strong in the grace that is in Christ Jesus, we need to understand very clearly God's unmerited favor for his people, unmerited mediation, unmerited sacrificed Lamb, unmerited forgiveness, unmerited reconciliation, unmerited justification, unmerited redemption, unmerited eternal life, unmerited love, unmerited fellowship, unmerited reunion, so when you and I find ourselves progressively sinning, by an act of ignorance, shortcomings, faults and failures, or flat-out immaturity we need to realize that precious grace that was bestowed upon us by that lovely heavenly father through Jesus Christ, and in it we can be strong.

The apostle Paul is saying that the things which Timothy that already heard, to entrust and share it with faithful men not, only to apply it to their lives but to also teach it to other people.

Understand that all of these things that the apostle Paul is saying to Timothy we are able to put to practice in our own personal lives, and teach it to other faithful men, and to also suffer hardship as a soldier just like he was suffering for the cost of Christ.

Now the apostle Paul said to him that if you're going to be a soldier and be enlisted in the Army of God, you cannot be entangled with the affairs of everyday life, so that we may please the one who enlisted us.

Notice how the apostle Paul is considering a person or persons were involved in the body of Christ, as soldiers, and as athletes.

On verse five he says that in order to compete as an athlete and win we must do it by the rules, and then he goes on to say that a hard-working farmer needs to receive his fair share of the crops, in other words he needs to get paid for what he does in the farm.

So I can act, live, and enlist, like a soldier, or an athlete, in the Army of the Lord.

GOD SAYS, THAT I CAN, (BE A WORKMAN HANDLING THE WORD OF TRUTH)

In second Timothy chapter 2:14, 19 Remind them of these things, and solemnly charge them in the presence of God not wrangle about words, which is useless, and leads to the ruin of the hearers.

Verse 15, Be diligent to present yourself approved of God as a workman who does not need to be ashamed, handling accurately the word of truth.

Verse 16, But avoid worldly and empty chatter, for it will lead to further ungodliness.

Verse 17, and their talk will spread like gangrene. Among them are Hymenaeus and philetus,

Verse 18, then who have gone astray from the truth saying that the resurrection has already taken place, and thus they upset the faith of some.

Verse 19, Nevertheless, the firm foundation of God stands, having this seal, "The Lord knows those who are his." And "Let everyone who names the name of the Lord abstain from wickedness.

Here we see the apostle Paul coming Timothy to be entangled with hearsay so, and discussions against or in favor of the word, which he says it is useless and leads to the ruin of the hearers, and to be diligent to present ourselves approved as a workman that needs not to be ashamed, handling accurately the word of truth.

And for all of us to abstain from worldly chatter, which will lead to further ungodliness and it, will spread like gangrene just like our two brothers which we already read.

GOD SAYS, THAT I CAN, (PREACHED THE WORD IN SEASON, OUT OF SEASON)

In second Timothy chapter 4:1, 5 I solemnly charge you in the presence of God and of Christ Jesus, who is to judge the living and the dead, and by his appearing and his kingdom:

Verse two, preached the word; be ready in season and out of season; reprove, rebuke, exhort, with great patience and instruction.

Verse three, For the time will come when they will not endure sound doctrine; but wanting to have their ears tickled, they will accumulate for themselves teachers in accordance to their own desires;

Verse four, and will turn away their ears from the truth, and will turn aside to myths.

Verse five, But you, be sober in all things, endure hardship, do the work of an evangelist, fulfill your ministry.

God has called all of us to share, to preach, in and out of season, but we must do it with great patience and instruction, and to reprove, rebuke, and exhort the righteousness.

For he says that the time will come when they will not endure sound doctrine, but they will want their ears tickled, and they will accumulate to themselves teachers according to their desires, and not according to the words of God, they will turn their ears from the truth, and they will be believing myth's, horoscope's, oriental wisdom, and others.

GOD SAYS, THAT I CAN, (HEAR HIS VOICE THROUGH HIS SON)

In Hebrews chapter 1:1, 4 God, after he spoke long ago to the fathers in the prophets in many portions and in many ways,

Verse two, in these last days has spoken to us in his son, whom he appointed heir of all things, through whom also he made the world.

Verse three, And he is the radiance of his glory and the exact representation of that nature, and upholds all things by the word of his power. When he had made purification of sins, he sat down at the right hand of the Majesty on high;

Verse four, having become as much better than the Angels, as he has inherited a more excellent name than they.

In the Old Testament which are the first 39 books of the Bible, God spoke to people, through his prophets, through his ministers, and through the 10 Commandments.

On this #6 dispensation of grace which is the unmerited favor of God towards human beings, God speaks to us through Jesus Christ, every time we read the four Gospels, and we hear the teachings of Jesus Christ it is God through him speaking to us, when we go to Matthew's chapter 5:1,12.

Verse one, And when he saw the multitudes, he went up on the mountain; and after he sat down, his disciples came to him.

Verse two, And opening his mouth he began to teach them, saying,

Verse three, "Blessed are the poor in spirit, for theirs is the kingdom of heaven.

Verse four, "Blessed are those who mourn, for they shall be comforted.

Verse five, "Blessed are the gentle, for they shall inherit the earth.

Verse six, "Blessed are those who hunger and thirst for righteousness, for they shall be satisfied.

Verse seven, "Blessed are the merciful, for they shall receive mercy.

Verse eight, "Blessed are the pure in heart, for they shall see God.

Verse nine, "Blessed are the peacemakers, for they shall be called sons of God.

Verse 10, "Blessed are those who have been persecuted for the sake of righteousness, for theirs is the kingdom of heaven.

Verse 11, "Blessed are you when men cast insults at you, and persecute you, and say all kinds of evil against you falsely, on account of me.

Verse 12, "Rejoice, and be glad, for your reward in heaven is great, for so they persecuted the prophets who were before you.

Here we see Jesus Christ of Nazareth teaching his disciples after they had sat down before him and he started to teach them, and this is God Almighty speaking through Jesus Christ to our hearts, and mentioning nine times the word blessed.

When Jesus Christ said blessed are those that are poor in spirit, he knew that even born again believers, Holy Spirit filled people will go through a season of low spiritual communion with God, and that we should be rejoicing because the kingdom of God was ours.

I have never met a Christian in this world that has not mourn in their lives at least once or twice, but Jesus said be of good cheer because you will be comforted.

Every born-again Christian should be a gentle and kind individual, for in developing these qualities we will inherit the earth.

Jesus said that those who hunger and thirst after righteousness, which means right standing, right relationships with other people, treating others righteously, that we would inevitably be satisfied.

Jesus told us that we would be blessed if we were merciful to other people, because as we sow mercy in the lives of other people, we will receive mercy.

Jesus said blessed are the pure in heart, for they shall see God.

Jesus said blessed are the peacemakers, for they shall be called the sons of God, the people that are constantly practicing peaceful relationships, not the gossipers, not the troublemakers, not the fault finders, not the ungrateful, not the judgmental, not the critical, but the peacemakers.

Jesus said that we are blessed who have been persecuted for the sake of righteousness, for theirs is the kingdom of heaven, and in practicing righteousness, and in loving other people, and in preaching the gospel, and even leaving your Christian life, we will find persecution, for this righteous lifestyle that we are living, unbelievers, heaters of God, and haters of Christianity will always laugh at us, criticize us, call us holier than thou, and reject us because we have decided to follow Jesus, and not self-destruct in corruption like they are living, which is probably a religious lifestyle, or an ungodly lifestyle.

Jesus said blessed are you when men cast insults at you, and persecute you, and say all kinds of evil against you falsely, on account of me, we should always rejoice, and be glad for our reward is great in heaven, and on earth peace, goodwill, identity, and an inheritance bestowed upon us.

Now in the gospel of Matthew as we are about to read, Jesus Christ himself said that we are salt, and that we can give the proper flavor everywhere we go, because we bring the right ingredient to make things taste good, imagine, the salt of the earth, this is a powerful statement said by the mouth of Jesus Christ himself the son of the most high God, who is speaking through him, and to us, yes we will find persecution, but the Earth needs us.

Jesus Christ of Nazareth is the light of the world and there is no question about that, but when he said that we are the light of the world, it is understood that because the light leaves inside of us and we are his lampstand that is why we are considered to be the light.

We all know that a lamp does not have light, but it reflects the light that comes through the wire into the pole and finally into the light bulb that lights up and then gives light, and that is exactly the way we are, we are the lamp, Jesus is the light, and he reflects through us his nature, his love, his mercy, compassion, and his understanding.

In Matthew chapter 5:13, 16 "You are the salt of the earth; but if the salt has become tasteless, how will it be made salty again? It is good for nothing anymore, except to be thrown out and trampled underfoot by men.

Verse 14, "You are the light of the world. A city set on a Hill cannot be hidden.

Verse 15, "Nor do men light a lamp, and put it under the peck measure, but on the lampstand; and it gives light to all who are in the house.

Verse 16, "Let your light shine before men in such a way that they may see your good works, and glorify your father who is in heaven.

So you see we do hear the word of God, through Jesus Christ himself, and every single teaching, and every single preaching, and every single act of kindness and goodness that Jesus ever did belongs to us, and because he lives in us by the power of the Holy Spirit, we are everything Jesus says that we are, we have everything that Jesus says that we have, and we can do everything the Jesus says we can do, because after all it is God talking through Jesus just as we mentioned previously.

GOD SAYS I AM, GOD SAYS I HAVE, AND GOD SAYS I CAN, IN CHRIST:

Now it's important for us to recap so far what the word has been saying, after that we repented, after that we turn from our wicked ways, and after we invited Jesus to come into our hearts, he did come in and take up residence within by the Holy Spirit.

This is what God says I am, God says that I am, 1) a new creation, 2) God says that I am born of an incorruptible seed, 3) God says that I am born again, 4) God says that, I am spiritual babe, 5) God says that I am a child of God.

6) God says that I am delivered from the kingdom of darkness, and into the kingdom of his dear son, 7) God says that I am the righteousness of God in Christ. 8) God says that I am a member of Christ's body, 9) God says that I am a temple of the Holy Spirit, 10) God says that I am an ambassador for Christ, 11) God says that I am a chosen generation, 12) God says that I am a royal priesthood, 13) God says that I am a holy nation, 14) God says that I am a peculiar people, 15) God says that I am to show forth his praises, 16) God says that I am an heir and joint heir with Christ Jesus, and therefore a recipient of everything Jesus did on the cross on my behalf.

This is what God says I have, 1) God says that I have a full armor to my benefit, where I have a shield of faith, and the sword of the spirit which is the word of God, to quench every fiery dart of the enemy, 2) God says that I have a brand-new life, 3) God says that I have a new divine nature within me, 4) God says that I have a citizenship in heaven, 5) God says that I have been set free, from the power of the devil, 6) God says that I have his leadership for triumph, 7) God says I have a high priest and a mediator, 8) God says that I have a new covenant, 9) God says that I have been grafted into the rich root, 10) God says that I have a new confidence in him, 11) God says that I have a lawyer seated at the right hand of the Majesty to intercede for me in every area of my life, 12) God says that I have been given power, authority, in the name of Jesus against serpents and scorpions and over all the power of the devil, and nothing shall hurt me.

This is what God says I can, 1) God says I can do all things through Jesus Christ who strengthens me, 2) God says I can live worry free, 3) God says I can receive answers to my prayers, 4) God says I can fight the good fight of faith and win, 5) God says I can overcome the world, 6) God says I can walk in the spirit and not fulfill the lust of my flesh, 7) God says I can forgive other people, and myself, 8) God says I can cast all my cares upon him, because he cares for me, 9) God says I can renew my mind with the word of God, 10) God says I can know his wisdom, 11) God says I can find his will, and know his will, and do his will.

12) God says his will, is he's New Testament, and I should develop my identity, and my new Christian behavior, 13) God says his will, is his church, the body of Christ, and I should find my position in it, 14) God says that I can develop the prerequisite for Bishop, 15) God says that I can develop a prerequisite for a Deacon, 16) God says that I can develop the prerequisite for a minister, 17) God says that I can suffer like a soldier, and an athlete, 18) God says that I can be a workman handling the word of truth, 19) God says that I can preach his word in season and out of season, 20) God says that I can hear his voice through Jesus Christ his son, and be, and do everything he says, I can.

God says I am, God says I have, and God says I can:

There is literally hundreds of other things that we are in Christ under the new dispensation of grace, that we have in Christ under the new dispensation of grace, and that we can in Christ under the new dispensation of grace, but because of the sake of time, and the length of this book we are cutting it down from 12 to 20 attributes that were given to us on the cross thanks to the shed blood of Jesus Christ.

These attributes came with the person of Jesus Christ as he came inside our hearts to take his abode with us, and it is what he has made us to be, it's not the thought of a wild ridiculous person, who had nothing better to do, but it's according to Scriptures.

Romans chapter 12:2,3 And be not conformed to this world: but be ye transformed by the renewing of your mind, that you may prove what is that good, and acceptable, and perfect, will of God.

Verse three, For I say, through the grace given unto me, to every man that is among you, not to think of himself more highly than he ought to think; but to think soberly, according as God has dealt to every man the measure of faith.

At the beginning of this teaching I have already explained this chapter and verse, but for the sake of clarification I'm going do it again, Notice what it says on verse 2, be not conformed to this world, in other words do not think, speak, act, and develop a self-worth, self-value according to this world system, nor govern your affairs according to this world system, nor treat your brothers and sisters according to this world's system, our self-worth, our self-value, has to come from what Christ has done on the cross through his shed blood.

Now in Verse two, then he gives us a command of what we ought to do, and that is to be transformed, by the renewing of our minds, for unless we renew our minds, we do not get transformed, and we do not know God's acceptable and perfect, will.

Now, what we have to do is 1) Not to be conformed to this world, 2) To be transformed, 3) And it is done through the renewing of our mind, 4) That we may be able to prove, 5) God's acceptable and perfect will.

And in verse 3, Paul is speaking through the grace that was given unto him, to tell every brother that was among them not to think of himself more highly than he ought to think, but to think soberly,

According as God has dealt to every man the measure of faith.

I underlined not to think of him more highly than he (Ought to think), but to think soberly. Every born-again believer has a measure of faith deposited within us, and as we read the word of God, as we pass that information from our heads into our hearts, and as we make God's word a Part of our everyday life, we begin to be transformed, as we are renewing our minds.

So I'm Going to Say What God Says, That I Am, what God says that I have, and what God says that I can, and these are the keys to a healthy self-worth, a healthy self-value, and ultimately the development of my identity in Christ, which is truly what the devil fears, because once I know who I am in Christ, and what I have in Christ, and what I can do in Christ, then I rise from a negative self-image, from an unworthy self-image, from a poor old me syndrome mentality, from I will never reach any thing in life mentality, and defeat every negative thought, every fiery dart of the enemy, that the enemy has been throwing against me all of my life.

And defeat that rascal in every area of my life, through my thought life, my speech, my self-worth, my identity, thereby being transformed, and knowing God's acceptable, God's perfect will.

God wants us to know that we are members of Christ's body, the triumphant church of the Lord Jesus Christ, and we are his Bride washed in his precious blood without spot or wrinkle, he is the groom, and he is coming for his bride for the marriage supper of the Lamb waiting for us in heaven.

This is why the devil attacks the members of Christ's body, because they are the bride, and the enemy does not want us to know our victory, our identity, and our God-given power, in Jesus Christ's name, this way we won't rise up from a poor old me syndrome, and take our inheritance, put on the entire armor of God, and defeat the enemy in every area of his life, and his demons, cohosts.

What we think, can be influenced by what we see, or by what we hear, or by what others say about us, causing us to develop a negative thought life, a pattern for thinking, contrary to the word of Almighty God, thereby causing us to be mentally imprisoned.

When this pattern for thinking becomes a way of life, we start speaking doubt, unbelief, discouragement, negativism, start complaining about everything, we start complaining about everybody, discontent sets in, and we become irritable, weary, disillusioned, and ultimately we become depressed, we see no way out.

I have met a lot of people, very good people, God fearing people, that are imprisoned in their minds, and they are the most an happy people in this planet, if this describes you reading this book right now, say this prayer with me out loud, heavenly father I come to you in Jesus name, asking you to forgive me, asking you to cleanse me with the precious blood of Jesus, deliver my four head, deliver my subconscious, cleanse my mind with the blood of Jesus, destroy every tormenting demon that torments my mind, I bow to give you honor, I bow to give you praise, I worship and I magnify you, please heavenly father as I surrender my will to yours help me to renew my mind with your word, and start saying what God says that I am, what God says that I have, and what God says that I can in Jesus Christ, that I may be transformed by the renewing of my mind, and finally get to know your acceptable, and perfect will in Jesus name, amen.

Always remember that when you're in prayer you can raise both of your arms to the sky, in an attitude of surrender ness, and call upon the blood of Jesus Christ to cleanse you, you can apply the blood of Jesus to your four head, to your conscience, to your back area, you can lay hands on your stomach, you can lay hands on your chest, you can lay hands on any part of your body and ask God in Jesus name to cleanse you, and to deliver you, and to break every yoke of bondage that is in slaving any part of your being, and he promised to set us free, you can also apply the blood of Jesus Christ on the door posts through prayer, on every window, and the blood of Jesus to build a hedge of protection around your home, and around your childrens mind, and room's.

In my own personal life there are things I won't think negative about, 1) God promised me 70 to 80 years of life, 2) God promised me an inheritance, 3) God promised me that I was an heir and a joint heir with Christ, 4) God promised me total and absolute deliverance, 5) God promised me that I have his seed living within me, 6) God promised me a new heart, 7) God promised me a renewed spirit, 8) God promised me a new life, 8) God promised me freedom from the power of the enemy over my life, 9) God promised me that I am a member of Christ's body, 10) God promised me that I was inserted into the rich root of the Jewish Commonwealth, 11) God promised me that through Christ I was the seed of Abraham, 12) God promised me that through Christ I was more than a conqueror, 13) God promised me that since I was his temple, My body would be healthy, 14) God promised me that I would inherit the riches of this world so that he could established his covenant with me, and with my children, and with my children's children, 15) God promised me that I would overcome every obstacle the enemy would ever throw against me, 16) God promised me triumph and victory over the world, 16) God promised me a sound mind, 17) God promised me a covenant, found in his new testament, of which I am an heir of, 18) God promised me that I would inherit everything that the New Testament says it's mine.

God promised that I can fight the good fight of faith and win, 19) God promised me that I was the blood bought, blood cleansed, victorious body of Christ, and that the Gates of hell would not prevail against the church of the living Christ, 20) And last but not least God promised me excellency in spirit, excellency in mind, excellency in my body, excellency with the law, excellency with my finances, excellency for my marriage, excellency for my family, and excellency for my children and their children, and I will not settle for second best, or anything less than what I just mentioned, and for these blessings I will fight the good fight of faith every single day of my life in Jesus Christ name, amen.

Let's look at what God says, that I should do in Christ:

THE # 1 THING I SHOULD DO IN CHRIST: (LOVE)

In the gospel of Matthew chapter 22:34, 40 But when the Pharisees heard that he had put the Sadducees to silence, they gathered themselves together.

Verse 35, And one of them, a lawyer, asked him a question, testing him,

Verse 36, "Teacher, which is the great commandment in the law?"

Verse 37, And he said to him, "You shall love the Lord your God with all of your heart, and with all of your soul, and with all of your mind.'

Verse 38, "This is the great and foremost commandment.

Verse 39, "The second is like it, 'You shall love your neighbor as yourself.'

Verse 40, "On these two commandments depend the whole law and the prophets."

On this particular teaching that Jesus gave the Pharisees about the new commandment, after silencing the Sadducees, one of them being a lawyer asked him a question in order to test him, about the commandment in the law, and Jesus answered to them as well as to us what exactly it is we need to be doing in regards to our lives.

You shall love the Lord your God with all of your heart, and with all of your soul, and with all of your mind, and this is the great and foremost commandment.

And the second is like it, 'You shall love your neighbor as yourself.'

The beauty about loving our heavenly father with all our heart, and with all of our soul, and with all of our mind, is that after being born again he has sealed, and baptized us with the Holy Spirit of promise, and one of the fruit of the Holy Spirit is love, so loving God with that same love, and our brethren should be easy for the born again believer. And of course we don't want to go to the first commandment which should be our priority, and undivided love for our heavenly father, but focus on the second commandment of which I want to put an emphasis on; (You shall love your neighbor as yourself.)

The first question I want to ask us is how much do we love ourselves? The second question I want to ask ourselves is, do we love ourselves enough to take care of us? Third question I want to ask is, do we love ourselves enough to do anything about renewing our minds? The fourth question I want to ask is, do we love ourselves enough to develop a spiritual communion with God, in order to heal our emotions? The fifth question I want to ask is, do we love ourselves enough to make special time in prayer with God? The sixth question I want to ask is, do we love ourselves enough to spend minimum 30 minutes a day through the reading of God's word? The seventh question I want to ask is, do we love ourselves enough to eat well, exercise, rest well? The eighth question I want to ask is, do we love ourselves enough to respect ourselves and stop thinking and talking negative words to ourselves and others?

The ninth question I want to ask is, do we love ourselves enough to live out our biblical godly convictions, and not be afraid to share our faith? And the 10th question I want to ask is, do we love ourselves enough to develop a plan of action, to make the necessary changes in our minds and our bodies, thereby developing a healthy self-worth, self-value and ultimately loving ourselves enough, in order to be content with ourselves, respect ourselves, that we would be ready to go out and love our neighbors as we love ourselves.

In the book of Proverbs chapter 23:7 For as he thinketh in his heart, so is he: Eat and drink, saith he to thee; but his heart is not with thee.

Jesus Christ of Nazareth came to set us free, to deliver us from an emotional instability, to give us a new heart, to heal our bad past experiences, to take away grief, to take away pain, take away sorrow, take away the torment, he came to set us free, Jesus Christ does not want us to be an emotional wreck, and the people that govern themselves according to their emotions, who are up-and-down, they are double minded and receive absolutely nothing from the Lord.

THE # 2 THING I SHOULD DO IN CHRIST. (NOT BE A VICTIM OF MY FLESH).

>In Galatians chapter 5:17 for the flesh lusts against the spirit, and the Spirit against the flesh: and these are contrary the one to the other: so that you cannot do the things that you would.
>
>In Galatians chapter 5:19 now the works of the flesh are manifest, which are these; adultery, fornication, uncleanness, lasciviousness,
>
>Verse 20, idolatry, witchcraft, hatred, variance, emulations, wrath, strife, seditions, heresies,
>
>Verse 21, Envying's, murders, drunkenness, raveling's, and such like: of the which I tell you before, as I have also told you in time past, that they which do such things shall not inherit the kingdom of God.

Likewise the people that are governed by their bodies, they can't stop eating, they cannot stop drinking, they cannot stop smoking, they cannot stop sleeping, they cannot stop resting, they have become couch potatoes, people who dream of food, and have uncontrollable craving for desserts and sugars of all sorts.

These people are totally unhappy about their lives, they speak doubt, they speak unbelief, they speak discouragement, they speak negativism, they are complaining about everything, they are complaining about everybody, they are irritable, they are judgmental, they are critical, they are condemning, they are controlling, they are the demeaning, they are verbally abusive, they are weary, they are disillusioned, they are unmotivated, they are discontent, they don't know what to do with their lives, and ultimately they will be depressed, and give up.

We are a spirit, possessing a soul, and living inside our body, it should be our spirit man in obedience to the written word of God that should govern our thought life, our bodies, and our destiny.

That's why the apostle Paul said in Romans chapter 12:1,2 I beseech you therefore, brethren, by the mercies of God, that you present your bodies a living sacrifice, holy, acceptable unto God, which is your reasonable service.

And be not conformed to this world: but be ye transformed by the renewing of your mind, that you may prove what is that good, and acceptable, and perfect will of God.

So we must love our God with all of our heart, with all our soul, and with all of our minds, and this is the first commandment.

And the second commandment is that we love our neighbor, as we love ourselves.

THE # 3 THING I SHOULD DO IN CHRIST, IS PRAYER: (MIND)

Let us pray right now, and say these words out loud with me, heavenly father I come to you in Jesus name, confessing to you that I have missed the mark for on emotionally stable thought life, and for that I ask you to forgive me, I ask you to cleanse me, I ask you to wash me with the precious blood of Jesus, destroy every work of the enemy in my thought life, take away every pattern of thinking that is self-destructive, help me to renew my mind with what you say that I am in Christ, with what you say that I have in Christ, with that what you say that I can in Christ, and help me to confess with my mouth your words that I have just read in this book about my healthy self-identity in Jesus name amen.

I also want to pray for the lust of the eye's, which is the gate way to your mind and ultimately to your flesh and its lusts, so say with me out loud heavenly father, I come to you in Jesus name, I ask you to deliver my mind from every influence of lustful desires, deliver my mind from oppressing spirits, from tormenting spirits, that are constantly bombarding my mind.

Wash me with your precious blood, deliver my subconscious, deliver my four head, deliver the top of my head, I apply the blood of Jesus to it, and set me free from everything contrary to the word of God.

Also deliver me from reading filthy material that hurt my communion with you, and with your help I will throw away every printed material that have to do with pornography, and close every door through the Internet, television, or printed material, that influences my mind and ultimately enslaves me, and keeps me away from you.

Heavenly father I also call upon the precious Holy Spirit to invade my home, my bedroom, my living room, hallway, bathroom's, garage area and complete property, invade my bedroom, where I rest and lift my arms to the sky and fellowship with you. Holy Spirit, I invite you fill my body, fill my mind, fill my entire being with your presence, and take control of my spirit soul and body in Jesus name.

THE # 4 THING I SHOULD DO IN CHRIST, IS PRAYER: (BODY)

Let us pray right now, and say these words out loud with me, heavenly father I come to you in Jesus name, according to Galatians chapter 3:13 father you have deliver me from the curse of the law, you have your seed inside my body, you have destroy the works of the devil over my life, you have deliver me from the legal right the devil had over my life, and you have set me free, your son Jesus Christ of Nazareth has taken away all my sickness, all my diseases, all my infirmities, and therefore whom the son sets free is free in deed, so precious heavenly father in the name of Jesus I thank you that you have made me a new creature, and that I am a child of the most high God, and thanks to the precious blood of Jesus on the cross, I am the righteousness of God in Christ, I am the temple of the Holy Spirit, I am an ambassador for Christ, I am a chosen generation, I am a Royal priesthood, I am a holy nation, and I am a peculiar people, therefore the enemy has no right to hold me in bondage in Jesus name.

Now precious heavenly father in Jesus name, fill me with the precious Holy Spirit, strengthen the hidden man of my heart, give me a double portion of your anointing, saturate my being with your precious Holy Spirit, destroy every single oppressing, influencing, and tormenting demon power that has been keeping me in bondage all these years, set me free father from the crown of my head to the soles of my feet, for I have become a godly property, I have been bought and paid for by the blood of Jesus, therefore I do not belong to the kingdom of darkness, I belong to the body of the Lord Jesus Christ, and of his flesh and off his bones, and the enemy has no legal right, the trespass against God's property, make me bold, strong, and courageous, to make changes and be spirit ruled, not emotional ruled, not physically ruled, but spiritually ruled in Jesus holy name I pray amen.

Wow, as I prayed this prayer I sensed the Holy Spirit of the living Jehovah God invade this entire office, and I'm saturated with his holy presence.

THE # 5 THING I SHOULD DO IN CHRIST, (LIVE THE NEW LIFE)

In the letter of Paul to the Romans chapter 6:15, 22 What then? Shall we sin, because we are not under law, but under grace? God forbid.

Verse 16, Now ye not, but to whom you yield your selves servants to obey, his servants ye are to whom you obey; whether of sin unto death, or of obedience unto righteousness?

Verse 17, But God be thanked, that ye were the servants of sin, but ye have obeyed from the heart that form of doctrine which was delivered you.

Verse 18, Being then made free from sin, ye became the servants of righteousness.

Verse 19, I speak after the manner of men because of the infirmity of your flesh: for ye have yielded your members servants to uncleanness and to iniquity unto iniquity; even so now yield your members servants to righteousness unto holiness.

Verse 20, For when you were the servants of sin, ye were free from righteousness.

Verse 21, What fruit had ye then in those things whereof ye are now ashamed? For the end of those things is death.

Verse 22, But now being made free from sin, and become servants to God, ye have your fruit unto holiness, and the end everlasting life.

Now the apostle Paul is saying to the people in Rome that because they are under the dispensation of grace, and not under the law, they should not continue in sin.

And that if we Christians submit ourselves to anything or anyone to obey that we would become servants of that which we submit ourselves to, whether sin unto death, or obedience unto righteousness.

Thank God we now have a choice, we don't have to be a victim of our thought life, and we don't have to be a victim of our flesh, and because we were made free from sin, we became servants of righteousness, and he was speaking after the manner of men because of their infirmity on their flesh, which because they submitted themselves as servants to uncleanness and iniquity they were all sick.

But now since we are all made free from sin, we have become servants of God, and we have fruit unto holiness, and the end there of is everlasting life.

So you see my brother and my sister thanks be unto Jesus, who while we were yet in sin he died for us, that we might become the righteousness of God in him.

We no longer have to be a victim of a negative thought life, or be fleshly governed any more, we can have victory over the eyes, victory over the flesh, and victory over the world, because in Jesus we are more than conquerors through him that loved us, amen.

In Colossians chapter 2:6, 12 As you have therefore received Christ Jesus the Lord, so walk ye in him:

Verse seven, Rooted and built up in him, and established in the faith, as ye have been taught, abounding therein with thanksgiving.

Verse eight, Beware lest any man spoil you through philosophy and vain deceit, after the tradition of men, after the rudiments of the world, and not after Christ.

Verse nine, for in him dwelleth all the fullness of the Godhead bodily.

Verse 10, And ye are complete in him, which is the head of all principality and power:

Verse 11, In whom also ye are circumcised with the circumcision made without hands, in putting off the body of the sins of the flesh by the circumcision of Christ:

Verse 12, Buried with him in baptism, wherein also ye are risen with him through the faith of the operation of God, who have raised him from the dead.

Every Christian should walk in newness of life, we have a brand-new life in Christ, we are a brand-new creature in Christ, and God is expecting us to walk the new life, the risen life, the Godly life that pleases him, because he said that we are built up in him, and established in the faith, and he is expecting us to be different from people in the world.

Then he warns us to be very careful about seducing spirits, which comes directly from the enemy to spoil us through philosophy and vain deceit, according to the traditions of our forefathers, that are after the rudiments of this world, and not after Christ, our responsibility in Christ is to walk according to his precepts, ideals, and methods, and not according to our vain traditions that contradict the word of God.

In Christ Jesus, dwelleth all the fullness of the Godhead bodily, which means God the father Creator, God the son redeemer, God the Holy Spirit sustainer, baptizer, giver of the fruit of the Holy Spirit, and giver of the gifts of the Holy Spirit, giving us a solid and good foundation which is the word of God, the covenant of God, the New Testament of God, to be built up upon, and we do not need to listen to, follow after, or submit to any other philosophy contrary to the holy word of God, to live a Godly life.

And every Christian in the world, that has confessed Jesus Christ as Lord over their lives, is complete in him, which is the head over all principalities and powers.

Every Christian in the world has a new circumcision, and that is not of the flesh, and it is done without hands, and thanks to it we have put off the sins of the flesh, thanks to the new circumcision of Christ.

Thanks to the operation of God's power, who raised Jesus Christ from the dead, who buried us with him in baptism, and raised us up with him through faith, every believer around the world has a resurrected life, therefore we can live a new Christian life, a new Christian resurrected life, with delegated authority, and power over all the works of the enemy, so that we can be the head and not the tail, so that we could be on top and not beneath, so that we can be the conqueror and not the victim. The new Christian identity, the new Christian life, the new life that God wants us to live it's not complicated or difficult, we just have to discover our identity, our rights and privileges, and our God-given power, that has been freely delegated to us through Christ. Thank God we are free to obey.

THE # 6 THING I SHOULD DO IN CHRIST, (PUT OFF THE OLD MAN)

Now in Colossians chapter 3:1, 9 If ye then be risen with Christ, seek those things which are above, where Christ is seated on the right hand of God.

Verse two, set your affection on things above, not on things on the earth.

Verse three, for ye are dead, and your life is hid with Christ in God.

Verse four, When Christ, who is our life, shall appear, then shall ye also appear with him in glory.

Verse five, Mortify therefore your members which are upon the earth; fornication, uncleanness, inordinate affection, evil concupiscence, and covetousness, which is idolatry:

Verse six, For which things sake' the wrath of God cometh on the children of disobedience:

Verse seven, in which ye also walked some time, when ye lived in them.

Verse eight, But now ye also put off all these; anger, wrath, malice, blasphemy, filthy communication out of your mouth.

Verse nine, Lie not one to another, seeing that ye have put off the old man with his deeds;

Because we have been raised with Christ and are seated in heavenly places with him, we can seek those things which are above, where Christ is seated at the right hand of God. Every one of us should set our affection on things that are above, and not of the things of this world, because we are dead with him, and our life is hid with Christ in God, therefore when he appears we will appear with him in glory, at the second coming after the rapture.

So in Christ we no longer have to be a victim of uncontrollable anger, of uncontrollable wrath, or have a malice heart, or be a blasphemous person, or be involved in filthy communication out of our mouths, we no longer have to lie, or use deceit to get our way, because in Christ we have already put off the old man with his deeds, and we should no longer fall prey to these outbursts, and earthly fleshly desires.

THE # 7 THING I SHOULD DO IN CHRIST, (PUT ON THE NEW MAN)

In Galatians chapter 3:10, 17 And have put on the new man, which is renewed in knowledge after the image of him that created him:

Now notice here, And have put on the new man, which is renewed in the knowledge after the image of him that created him, Christ in us the hope of glory, and because he is in us, we are able, and capable of putting on progressively the new man.

Verse 11, Where there is neither Greek nor Jew, circumcision nor circumcision, barbarian, Scythian, bond nor free: but Christ is all, and in all.

Verse 12, Put on therefore, as the elect of God, holy and beloved, bowels of mercies, kindness, humbleness of mind, meekness, long-suffering;

Verse 13, Forbearing one another, and forgiving one another, if any man have a quarrel against any: even as Christ forgave you, so also do ye.

Verse 14, And above all these things put on charity, which is the bond of perfectness.

Verse 15, And let the peace of God rule in your hearts, to the which also ye are called in one body; and be ye thankful.

Verse 16, That the word of Christ dwell in you richly in all wisdom; teaching and admonishing one another in psalms and hymns and spiritual songs, singing with grace in your hearts to the Lord.

Verse 17, And whatsoever ye do in word or deed, do all in the name of the Lord Jesus giving thanks to God and the father by him.

Because Christ is in all believers and through all of us, we have already put on the new man inside of us, and so we need to let that new man with his Godly deeds flow out of us, in relationship to other people, for there is neither Greek nor Jew, bond nor free, circumcision nor uncircumcision, barbarian or scythian, but Christ is all, and in all.

And because we are the elect of God, holy and beloved, we can put on the bowels of mercy, and we should put on kindness, humbleness of mind, long-suffering, we should forbear one another, and forgive just as Christ has forgiven us.

And because we are the elect of God, holy and beloved, we can put on charity, which is the bond of perfectness, and allow the peace of God to rule our hearts at all times, and thereby be thankful to Jesus Christ for all he has done on the cross on our behalf.

And because we are the elect of God, holy and beloved, we will let the word of Christ dwell in us richly in all wisdom, and thereby share it with everybody through psalms and hymns and spiritual songs, and we will always sing with grace in our hearts to the Lord.

And because we are the elect of God, holy and beloved, everything we do in word and deed, we will do it all in the name of the Lord Jesus giving thanks to God and the father by him. We are truly grateful and thankful to our heavenly father through Christ, we are able to put on the new man, and it is not as hard as I have heard preached in other circles, praise his holy name, hallelujah.

THE # 8 THING I SHOULD DO IN CHRIST, (WALK IN THE SPIRIT)

In the letter of Paul to the Galatians chapter 5:16, v 22, 26 This I say then, Walk in the spirit, and ye shall not fulfill the lust of the flesh.

Verse 22, But the fruit of the spirit is love, joy, peace, long-suffering, gentleness, goodness, faith,

Verse 23, Meekness, temperance: against such there is no law.

Verse 24, And they that are Christ's have crucified the flesh with the affections and lusts.

Verse 25, If we live in the spirit, let us also walk in the spirit.

Verse 26, Let us not be delirious of vain glory, provoking one another, envying one another.

As we Christians walk in love, as we walk in joy, as we walk in peace, as we walk in long-suffering, as we walk being gentle, as we walk in life being good to others, and full of faith, which that is walking in the spirit, I assure you, you will not fulfill the lust of the flesh.

It is important to understand that we who are Christians, we have crucified the flesh, with its affections and lusts, we no longer have to be a victim of it ever again, we can walk in obedience by the fruit of the spirit that was already deposited within us.

When we walk in the spirit, or the fruit of the spirit which we already mentioned, it guarantees us to be Christ like which is what we are supposed to be transformed into, the image of Jesus Christ, every born-again believer has to be transformed by the renewing of his mind, and that is to have Jesus Christ as your mirror in relationship to other people, and the question ought to be how would Jesus Christ act in a situation like this, how would Jesus Christ treat a person, or a child, or a husband, or a wife, how would he deal with the situation? And that is what walking in the spirit is my friend, my thought life, that my words, and that my conduct, in relationship to people ought to be Christ like.

So provoking one another, and envying one another, and being judgmental towards one another, being critical of the life of other people, or being a faultfinding person is obviously not walking in the spirit, but walking in the flesh.

Now loving God, and loving others as myself, not being a victim of the flesh, constantly praying for my mind, and praying for my body, living the new life in Christ, putting off the old man, learning to put on the new man, and walking in the spirit, so that I won't fulfill the lust of my flesh is a forever task, and it never stops, and it has absolutely nothing to do with God, and it has all to do with an act of obedience to the written word of God.

Always remembering that we are under a dispensation of grace, which is unmerited favor from God, and that we have an advocate with the father, the Lord Jesus, so when we fall, or when we come short of the mark of the high calling in Christ, every single believer in this planet will ignorantly, unintentionally, and for many reasons sin, we will never practice it, because we love the Lord enough to abstain, and to sanctify ourselves from this world's system, and to obey his word, but we will always sin.

THE # 9 THING I SHOULD DO IN CHRIST, (CONFESS OUR SINS, DAILY)

Now this is found in first John chapter 1:8, 10 If we say that we have no sin, we are deceiving ourselves, and the truth is not in us.

Verse nine, If we confess our sins, he is faithful and righteous to forgive us our sins and to cleanse us from all unrighteousness.

Verse 10, If we say that we have not sinned, we make him a liar, and his word is not in us.

In first John chapter 2:1, 4 My little children, I am writing these things to you that you may not sin. And if anyone sins, we have an advocate with the father, Jesus Christ the righteous;

Verse two, and he himself is the propitiation for our sins; and not for ours only, but also for those of the whole world.

Verse three, And by this we know that we have come to know him, if we keep his commandments, And remember there are only two that we have already talked about.

Verse four, The one who says, "I have come to know him," and does not keep his commandments, is a liar, and the truth is not in him;

Verse five, but whoever keeps his word, in him the love of God has truly been perfected. By this we know that we are in him:

And as we chaired already positionally,1) We are what God says We are, 2) We have what God says We have, 3) We can what God says We can, and progressively which is the development of what we are, have, and can in Christ, it could take all of our lives, which God New under this dispensation of grace, which is unmerited favor, we would be imperfect, we would be immature, we would fall, we would sin, and fall short of the mark.

Now in the process of keeping his commandments, it is guaranteed that we will be imperfect and fall short and sin, it never guaranteed that we would be perfect progressively, it only guaranteed that we would be perfect position ally. Thank God that his precious blood shed on Calvary's cross covered our past sin, are present sin, and our future sin, and we have an advocate on a daily basis at the right hand of the father interceding for us, as our heavenly lawyer, isn't that glorious? Isn't that spectacular?

So you see my brother and my sister keeping his commandments are easy for the born again believer, love God, and love your fellow man as you love yourself, and in this you have fulfilled the new commandment.

So for those Christians who keep his word, and abide by the written Scriptures, in him the love of the father has been perfected, and by this they will all know that we are in him.

THE # 10 THING I SHOULD DO IN CHRIST, (CONFESS OUR FAULTS)

In James chapter 5:16, Therefore, confess your sins to one another, and pray for one another, so that you may be healed. The effective prayer of a righteous man can accomplish much.

When two little children fight with each other, they give each other tantrums, but when two adults argue, disagree with something, or get angry with each other, the only biblical way to remedy this situation is confessing their faults to one another, but still I see to this day adults giving each other tantrums, just like little kids, they haven't learned the art of confessing their faults, because they don't admit faults, and they are thinking, talking, and acting just like people in the world, and this should not be.

I know that in my own personal relationships in life, I have dealt with people who are afraid to admit their faults and failures, and they are constantly justifying them, and constantly telling me why what they have done is justifiable in the eyes, and then when I let them know gently and compassionately with love that what they are doing is not biblical, they turn around and say why are you judging me. We should all be evaluating our thought life, our talk life, our believing life, and are acting life, by the reflection of Jesus Christ himself, are we saying it, are we doing it, and are we acting Christ like, and if we are not, we should be humble enough to come to our brothers and sisters and say look brother I'm sorry I made a mistake would you forgive me, and that should be the end of it.

In our spiritual growth, and in our transformation by the renewing of our minds, if we still have a sin conscience, and not a righteousness conscience, we are still babes in Christ, and we have not matured at all, and we have not grown in the knowledge of him who set us free, and have not developed an identity, a self-worth, a self-value, or a self-esteem according to Scriptures.

THE # 11 THING I SHOULD DO IN CHRIST, (BE HUMBLE)

In James chapter 4:6,7 But he gives a greater grace. Therefore it says, "God is opposed to the proud, but he gives grace to the humble."

Verse seven, Submit therefore to God. Resist the devil and he will flee from you.

As we said earlier, humility is obeying, thinking, talking, and doing the will of God which is the word of God, proud fullness is not obeying, thinking, talking, and not doing the will of God, believing something about ourselves that has nothing to do with the word of God, constitutes us as proud full people, but when we humble ourselves, and submit therefore to God by obeying his word, and we resist the devil and his lies, he has to flee from us, and his seductive and unbiblical views and ways about us dissipate completely.

So in other words humbling ourselves, and obeying the word of God, and resisting the devil's lies, causes God to give us greater grace.

THE # 12 THING I SHOULD DO IN CHRIST, (NOT JUDGE A BROTHER)

In James chapter 4:11, 12 Do not speak against one another, brethren. He who speaks against a brother, or judges his brother, speaks against the law, and judges the law; but if you judge the law, you are not a doer of the law, but a judge of it.

Verse 12, There's only one lawgiver and judge, the one who is able to save and to destroy; but who are you who judge your neighbor?

In the last 30 years of relating to Christians, I have noticed a continual situation with people not being humble enough to confess their faults to one another, or even coming to me and saying, my brother I'm sorry I have done you wrong would you forgive me? On the contrary, every single time I have questioned a situation, all I have gotten is a justifiable reasons why they have done what they've done, and even getting angry at me for even questioning the issue, as if they were perfect and never sinned in their whole life.

Now because I'm the kind of person that will never judge you, or correct you, or instruct you unless you ask me, when they see that I don't say anything about their behavior, they're under the impression that I'm in agreement with what they're saying, thinking, and doing, and it's not so, only because I respect them enough, to not judge them, and to not criticize them, doesn't necessarily mean that I'm in agreement with everything they are thinking, saying, or doing.

I'm also not going to say anything, judge anyone, or speak against any one of them, I'm just going to let them be, until they come to me for a question, or for prayer, I definitely do not want to be a judge of the law; I should be about doing the law and not judging it.

THE # 13 THING I SHOULD DO IN CHRIST, (NOT BE PARTIAL)

In James chapter 5:1,6, Come now, you rich, weep and howl for your miseries which are coming up on you.

Verse two, Your riches have rotted and your garments have become moth eaten.

Verse three, Your gold and your silver have rusted; and the rust will be a witness against you and will consume your flesh like fire, it is in the last days that you have stored up your treasure!

Verse four, Behold, the pay of the laborers who mowed your fields, and which has been withheld by you, cries out against you; and the outcry to those who did the harvesting has reached the ears of the Lord of Sabbath.

Verse five, You have lived luxurious on the earth and led a life of wanton pleasure; you have fattened your hearts in the day of slaughter.

Verse six, You have condemned and put to death the righteous man; he does not resist you.

Every person who puts their trusts in silver and gold will weep and howl because there misery will come upon them, because their riches have rotted, and their garments are moth eaten, and their gold and silver has rusted away, and it is that rusted away that has been witness against them, and it will consume their flesh like fire.

I have been in many churches where I see the pastor welcoming the people that have a lot of silver and gold, luxurious clothing, and in some instances careers, and political positions in the government, and they are given the best seats in the front of the church, while the raggedy person, or the person without a suit, or the person without a lot of money, are seated in the middle of the church, or at the end, I see a tremendous partiality everywhere I go around the world, and that is not what it ought to be the body of the Lord Jesus Christ.

These people that are given the best seat in the church, our exploiters of people, they are judgmental, they are critical, they Lord over their people, and they even withhold their pay, to the point where even these workers cannot even complain because if they do they get fired, and I see this all the time, and when they go to church they are given the royalty treatment, this high-minded self-exulting, and arrogant attitude is being welcomed in our churches as if they were God in person, they are not even preached the gospel to get saved as if they had a perfect relationship with God Almighty, and this is an abomination to God himself.

We should never show partiality, on the contrary you should treat the one without a suit, that one without good clothing, that one without the greatest amount of jewelry, with love, with respect, with acceptance, as your own personal blood brother, because this is the will of God, we should always vote for what is right, what is good, and what is righteously accepted by God.

THE # 14 THING THAT I SHOULD DO IN CHRIST, (I SHOULD MATURE)

Now in this particular topic there's a lot of controversy, because people just want to receive Christ into their hearts, received the baptism in the Holy Spirit, go to church on Sundays, develop a religious connotation to Christianity, but denying the transformation.

The transformation requires three major important steps, because as we already said earlier we are a new creation, with a new heavenly father, in a new family, the corporate body of Christ with a particular function we must discover and operate in.

Now I'm going to take you to three different Scriptures, that talks about our childhood spiritual state in relationship to our heavenly father.

The first scripture is found in second Corinthians chapter 5:17 Therefore if any man is in Christ, he is a new creature; the old things passed away; behold, new things have come.

The second Scriptures found in first Peter chapter 2:1, 2 Therefore, putting aside all malice and all guile and hypocrisy and envy and all slander,

Verse two, like newborn babe's, long for the pure milk of the word, that by it you may grow in respect to salvation,

Verse three, if you have tasted the kindness of the Lord.

The third Scripture is found in first Corinthians chapter 3:1, 4 And I, brethren, could not speak to you as to spiritual men, but as to men of flesh, as to babes in Christ.

Verse two, I gave you milk to drink, not solid food; for you were not yet able to receive it. Indeed, even now you are not yet able,

Verse three, for you are still fleshly. For since there is jealousy and strife among you, are you not fleshly, and are you not walking like mere men?

Verse four, For when one says, "I am of Paul," and another, "I am of Apollo's," are you not mere men?

Now on the first Scriptures when the Bible says if any man be in Christ he is a new creature, a new creation, all things have passed away, behold, new things have come.

This truly means that us being a new creation, or a new creature, we have no past anymore, in other words are old way of thinking, our old way of talking, and our old way of living, has passed away, behold, a new way of thinking, a new way of talking, and a new way of behaving has come, we are born into God's family, as new babes in Christ.

That is why the apostle Paul said, putting aside everything that our fleshly desires wants to do, which is malice, and guile, and hypocrisy, and envy, and all slander, like newborn babe's for us to long for the sincere milk of the word, that by it we would grow in respect to salvation. Now of course that is if we have tasted the kindness of the Lord, which means if we are saved.

Out of the third Scripture notice when the apostle Paul spoke, he said brother and I could not speak unto you as spiritual men, but as to men of flesh, as to babes in Christ, now there's a huge difference between a spiritual person, and a person that has not been born again yet, for the natural man receives not the things of the spirit, for they are foolishness unto him and he cannot discern them. 1corint2:14.

The apostle Paul said that he gave them milk to drink, not solid food, for they were not able to receive it, like a lot of people who are not able to receive solid biblical food.

Even now ye are not able to receive it, which is just like a lot of Christians today that are not able to receive solid biblical food, because they are still fleshly.

How do we really know that we are fleshly Christians? Very simple, let's look at the end of the verse three, For since there is jealousy and strife among you, are you not fleshly, and are you not walking as mere men? Their constant argument about who was their spiritual mentor whether it be Apollo's, or Paul, kept them in constant debate, the same apostle Paul had to call them mere men, and we Christians, who are born-again, Holy Spirit filled, are not mere men, we are spiritual babes, we are new creations, we are created beings, learning to stop being jealous, having strife in our lives, and having all kinds of fleshly desires operating in us.

THE # 15 THING I SHOULD DO IN CHRIST, (KNOW WHY I SHOULD MATURE)

The number one reason why I should mature in Christ is found.

In the book of Romans chapter 12:2 and do not be conformed to this world, but be ye transformed by the renewing of your mind, that you may prove what the will of God is, that which is good, and acceptable, and perfect, will of God.

There are four things here that we need to see very clearly, and the number one is to not be conformed to this world, conformed to this world means constantly operate in the method, in the views, in the value system of this world, not to operate in it anymore.

And the second thing I want us to see here is why we need to be transformed, the transformation that needs to take place in our attitude, in our way of thinking, and in our way of acting, that perfect reflection of the new life, is Jesus Christ himself, he is our mirror, so when we treat a human being we need to ask ourselves how would Jesus Christ himself treat him, how would Jesus Christ judge him, how would Jesus Christ love him, how would Jesus Christ encourage and motivate him, and this is the transformation that were changing from glory to glory to be Christ like.

The third thing I want us to see here is how this transformation will take place? The Only way this transformation will take place, is if we take everything you have been reading in this book, and you meditate on it so that it will become a reality in your heart and not a head knowledge, and when this information has passed from your head down into your heart, then you will look more and more like Jesus in your way of thinking, in your way of talking, and in your way of behaving which is our ultimate goal, to demonstrate the love, to demonstrate the compassion, the demonstrate the mercy, and to demonstrate the understanding of Jesus to a lost and dying world.

Now the fourth thing I want us to see here is why this transformation is a necessity, and we should not treat it like an option, we must be transformed by the renewing of our minds, so the end thereof may be, that we may prove, what the will of God is, which is good, and acceptable, and perfect.

The transformation is part of the maturity, part of the development of our relationship with God through Christ, and without it we will not be able to know the will of God, which is good, and acceptable, and perfect, so many Christians have asked me I don't know what the will of God is for my life, and they treat their spouses, and their children, and their moms and dads, with discontent, with anger, with bitterness, with resentment, we judged mental attitudes, they don't display a little bit of love towards other people, they are looking for a ministry to go out into the highway and byways around the world's to preach the gospel of Jesus Christ, and the simplest of all things they have not developed, which is an attitude that pleases God, that pleases your family members, and that reflects the salvation of the new life of Christ within us.

The second reason why I should mature in Christ is found.

In the epistle to the Ephesians chapter 4:11, 16 And he gave some, apostles; and some, prophets; and some, evangelists; and some, pastors and teachers;

These fivefold ministry gifts are the government of the Lord Jesus Christ within the local church; these are the five ministry gifts that ought to be teaching us and preaching to us, so that from verse

12 to verse 15 we may now why Jesus Christ himself put them as government within the church, I will talk more about them later on.

And on verse 12, For the perfecting of the saints, for the work of the ministry, for the edifying of the body of Christ:

Verse 13, Till we all come in the unity of the faith, and of the knowledge of the son of God, unto a perfect man, unto the measure of the stature of the fullness of Christ:

Verse 14, That we henceforth be no more children, tossed to and fro, and carried about with every wind of doctrine by the sleight of men, and cunning craftiness, whereby they lie in wait to deceive;

Verse 15, But speaking the truth in love, may grow up into him in all things, which is the head, even Christ:

Verse 16, From whom the whole body fitly joined together and compacted by that which every joint supplieth, according to the effectual working in the measure of every part, maketh increase of the body unto the edifying of itself in love.

As we very well may see Jesus Christ does not do anything in vain, everything he does has a purpose, and if we haven't paid much attention to anything we have read so far, please take notes from verse 12 to verse 15 where it clearly gives us the purpose.

For the perfecting of the Saints, we need to be perfected in our new walk, in our new life, within the local body of Christ, because we are the sanctified members of the body of Christ, we are the set aside one's, and we are called Saints.

That way we can do the work of the ministry within the body of Christ, for the edifying of the body, that is why we need to be perfected.

On verse 13, till we all come in the unity of the faith, Romans 12:3 says that we have been given a measure of faith, and that measure needs to grow up so that every one of us in the body of Christ may be united by that same measure of faith.

On that same verse 13, and of the knowledge of the son of God, unto a perfect man, onto the measure of the stature of the fullness of Christ.

On the same verse notice the word knowledge of the son of God, not everybody within the body of Christ has the same knowledge of the son of God, and that is why the fivefold ministry gifts were set in the body of Christ.

Onto a perfect man, a Godly man, a Christ like man, onto a being renewed man, maturing in that Christ likeness of our attitude towards people, onto the measure of the stature of the fullness of Christ, there is a stature of the fullness of Christ that I need to measure up to, thereby grow and mature to that stature.

And on verse 14, So that we will not be children, tossed to and fro, and carried about with every wind of doctrine. Sometimes on Sunday morning when I don't go to preach in someone's church I turn on the television and see every single kind of doctrine being taught over the television, and every single message totally different from the other, telling me to do something different, asking me to participate in something different, and trying to get me involved with every single ministry and it's flat out impossible.

We should not be children tossed to and fro, and carried about with every wind of doctrine, and this is why I wrote this book, so that we can renew our minds, not be led by our flesh, and be a disciple of Jesus Christ, with a solid biblical and healthy identity about ourselves in Christ, so that we may have a solid and healthy outlook on Christianity.

There is a lot of craftiness in pulpit's today whereby they lie in wait to deceive many that are not transformed by the renewing in their minds, who have not passed from childhood in Christ, to adult hood in Christ, who have not perfected their walk in Christ, people that don't even read the Bible for themselves, and are constantly being led astray and deceived in the knowledge of Christ.

On verse 15, but speaking the truth in love, may grow up into him in all things, which is the head, even Christ. Notice the word grow up it to him.

Now on verse 16, every member of the body of Christ should be fitly joined together, and compacted by that which every joint supplieth.

According to the effectual working in the measure of every part. Maketh increase of the body onto the edifying of itself in love.

Notice what it says here this is vitally important, that all of us should be fitly joined together, and compacted by that which every member brings to the table, which every joint supplieth, now please if you haven't understood many things remember that as a member of the body of Christ you have a part to play, and that part, is according to the effectual working in the measure of every part, when God saved us through Jesus Christ, he put within us a measure of an effectual working that only us, we can supply to the body of Christ.

Every one of us has talents, and abilities, and a God given part to play within the body of Christ, and as we turn over these talents and abilities, and our wills to God he will reveal to us what part within the body of Christ we should play, and till we operate in that member position within the body of Christ we will never find happiness, and be content about our salvation and calling.

The third reason why I should mature in Christ is found.

In Galatians chapter 3:28,29 There is neither Jew nor Greek, there is neither bond nor free, there is neither male nor female; for ye are all one in Christ Jesus.

Verse 29, And if ye be Christ's, then are ye Abraham's seed, and heirs according to the promise.

In Galatians chapter 4:1,7 Now I say, that the heir, as long as he is a child, differeth nothing from a servant, though he be Lord of all;

Verse two, But is under tutors and governors until the time appointed of the father.

Verse three, Even so we, when we were children, were in bondage under the elements of the world:

Verse four, But when the fullness of the time was come, God sent forth his son, made of a woman, made under the law,

Verse five, to redeem them that were under the law, that we might receive the adoption of sons.

Verse six, And because you are sons, God has sent forth the spirit of his son into your hearts, crying Abba father.

Verse seven, Wherefore thou art no more a servant, but a son; and if a son, then an heir of God through Christ.

In Christ there is neither Jew nor Greek, bond or free, there is neither male nor female, but we are all one in Christ.

And if we are Christ's, then we are Abraham's seed, and we are heirs according to the promise, so Everything God promised Abraham belongs to us, and we are heirs of it, that's why we have a new testament, a new covenant, God's holy word, where our inheritance has been written, and it's the source for the renewal of our mind's, as we mature in Christ, as we become perfected in Christ, every single one of his promises belong to us, and we have already dealt with how rich and powerful in livestock in knowledge and in cattle and in gold and silver Abraham was, and it all belongs to us, because God says we are heirs of Abraham.

Now there is a prerequisite here in order for us to be a partaker of that inheritance, and that is found in chapter 4:1 now the apostle Paul is trying to explain to us that an heir over a supernatural inheritance as long as he's a child, even though he is Lord over all of it, and over all principalities and powers and rules of this dark age, is no different than a servant or a slave, another translation says he does not differ at all from a slave although he is the owner of everything, the owner of everything, the recipient of the promises.

If we are spiritual babes, if we are a child in Christ, if we have not matured in Christ, if we have not been perfected in Christ, then it matters not that were saved, it matters not that we are holy spirit filled, we are no different from a non-born again, a carnal Christian, or a religious Christian, we cannot receive the inheritance that God left for us through the shed blood of Jesus Christ on the cross, written on a holy new testament, yes we will go to heaven, yes we are heaven bound, but we're living in barely get by street, afraid of the devil, running from the devil, with psychological bondage, and physiological bondage, being led by an emotionally unstable thought life, being led by our flesh, and it's desires, and having sickness and infirmity on our bodies like any other unbeliever in the world, we differ nothing from a nonbeliever.

Know that Jesus Christ of Nazareth defeated death, hell, and the grave, he came to undo the works of the devil, he came to shed his blood on the cross to pay the ran some, to purchase us from the legal right the enemy had over our lives, to give us a new heart, putting the Holy Spirit within us, translating us from the horrible dark Kingdome of the devil's domain over our lives, and inserting us into the rich root of the vine, the Commonwealth of Israel, and inserting us into the corporate body of Christ, and giving us a new spiritual rebirth into the family of God making us a child, and giving us the opportunity to mature, to develop a spiritual growth, so that we can inherit our inheritance.

It is very sad to see Christians in barely get by street, totally depressed, in total bondage, with no hope, with no direction, and not a drop of joy in their hearts, and it breaks my heart. This is why it says on verse three even so we, when we were children, were in bondage under the elements of the world:

Look at what it says on verse four, But when the fullness of the time was come, God sent forth his son, made of a woman, made under the law,

Verse five, To redeem them that were under the law, or any ritual that any Gentile has done or is doing, that we might receive the adoption of sons,

Verse six, And because we are sons, God has sent forth the spirit of his son into our hearts, crying Abba father. We are no more servants, we are no longer natural people, we are no longer slaves, we are sons of the Almighty God, he cares for us, he wants us to live in abundance, he wants us to have prosperity, he wants us to be the head, he doesn't want us to be the tail, he wants

us to be victorious, he wants us to overcome every fiery dart of the enemy, this is why he gave us the shield of faith, he wants us to use the sword of the spirit which is the word of Almighty God speaking, believing, acting upon, the word of Almighty God, to be an heir and joint heir with Christ of these promises, and not just waiting on tomorrow for something to happen, acting upon the written word of God to develop a healthy biblical -identity, a healthy self-esteem, a healthy self-worth, and a healthy self-value.

God does not want us to wait any longer, God wants us to believe in his written word, God wants us to have faith in our biblical identity in him, and no longer be a slave, or a servant, but to act upon the royalty that is within us, thanks to the seed of God planted within us, thanks to the holy nation he has made us, thanks to the peculiar people he has made us, thanks to the body of Christ he has made us, thanks to the temple of God he has made us, and many other things that we are in Christ.

We are no longer servants, we are no longer slaves, but we are sons of God, and heirs according to the promise, hallelujah we should be shouting and screaming and saying praise the Lord.

These are some of the things that we need to be doing in order to develop a healthy Outlook about ourselves, because according to the Scriptures we are just, and the just shall live by faith.

THE # 16 THING I SHOULD DO IN CHRIST, (NOT BE FRIENDS WITH THE WORLD)

In James chapter 4:4 ye adulterers and adulteresses, know ye not that the friendship of the world is enmity with God? Whosoever therefore will be a friend of the world is the enemy of God.

Now the Bible says that we are in this world, but we are not of this world for we already chaired that our citizenship is in heaven, and we are just passing through this world, now we're not talking about traveling, vacationing, enjoying ourselves, and many other things that we can do in this world.

Its talking about the system that operates in this world, which we already talked in prior chapters of this book and its found in first John chapter 2:16, 17 for all that is in the world, the lust of the flesh, the lust of the eyes, and the pride of life, is not of the father, but as of the world.

Verse 17, and the world passes away, and the lust thereof; but he that doeth the will of God abide forever.

I should not be friends with anything that seduces my life through the lust of the eyes, I should not be friends with anything in this world that seduces my life through the flesh, I should not be friends with anything in this world that seduces my life through the pride of life, because all these things do not come from the father, but are of the world, and the world passes away and its lusts thereof, but he that does the will of God will abide forever, isn't that glorious, hallelujah.

This Is why it starts with know ye not that the friendship with the world is enmity with God, whosoever therefore is a friend with the world is the enemy of God, if you are a victim of the lust of your eyes, or a victim of the lust of the flesh, or a victim of the pride of life, definitely you are not in fellowship with God, and you will never be able to inherit the promises of God through faith and patience.

The system of this world has a lot to do with self-indulgence, self-gratification, party all you can today, eat food, be Mary, and be happy, and that is enmity with God.

THE # 17 THING I SHOULD DO IN CHRIST, (LEARN GOD'S ECONOMY)

It is called the law of sowing and reaping found in.

Malachi chapter 3:7, 12 Even from the days of your fathers ye are gone away from mine ordinances, and have not kept them. Return on to me, and I will return unto you, saith the Lord of hosts. But ye said, Wherein he shall we return?

Verse eight, Will a man rob God? Yet ye have robbed me. But ye say, Wherein have we robbed thee? In tithes and offerings.

Verse nine, Ye are cursed with a curse; for ye have robbed me, even this whole nation.

Verse 10, Bring ye all the tithes into the storehouse, that there may be meat in mine house, and prove me now herewith, saith the Lord of hosts, if I will not open you the Windows of heaven, and pour you out a blessing, that there shall not be room enough to receive it.

Verse 11, And I will rebuke the devourer for your sakes, and he shall not destroy the fruits of your grown; neither shall your vine cast her fruit before the time in the field, saith the Lord of hosts.

Verse 12, And all the nations shall call you blessed: for ye shall be a delightsome land, saith the Lord of hosts.

Here we see God himself talking to the people through the prophet saying to them, even from the day of your fathers you have gone away from my ordinances, and have not kept them, and he is saying to them so that we should return unto him, and he will return on to us, and sometimes we ask where in shall we return.

God is saying whether Jews or Gentiles we have all robbed him, and if we are not tithing or offering in the church we are robbing God. We all know that the tithes is 10% of our net income and it is brought into the store house, the church, and offerings is any amount of money you want to give into the ministry for any costs within the local body of Christ or any other ministries around the world.

What God needs his food in his storehouse, that his priests, that his ministers, that his laypeople may be able to eat, and in today's terminology all the bills may be paid, and then he goes on to say prove me now, it's the only part of the entire Bible in all 66 books where God says prove me now herewith saith the Lord of hosts, if I will not open you the Windows of heaven, and pour you out a blessing that you will not have room enough to receive it, in another translation it says and I will open up the floodgates of heaven and pour you out a blessing you will not be able to contain.

And one of the parts that I like the most is where he says he will rebuke the devourer for ourselves, so that he will not destroy the fruits of our ground, or the fruit of our labor, or the fruit of our hard work, and the ultimate goal for this is all the nations of this world will see that we are blessed because we saw tithes and we give offerings to the church of the Lord Jesus Christ.

But you may say oh pastor but this is Old Testament, and we are under the new dispensation of grace, and you are absolutely right, under this new dispensation of grace we do not have to give 10%, because we belong to him completely, our spirit, our soul, our body, our finances, our homes, everything that we have Was given to us by God and he is the owner of everything and we are only the Stewarts of it, the managers of it. In the word to God.

In the book of acts chapter 4:32, 37 And the multitude of them that believed were of one heart and of one soul: neither said any of them that ought of the things which he possessed was his own; but they had all things common.

Verse 33, And with great power gave the apostles witness of the resurrection of the Lord Jesus: and great grace was upon them all.

Verse 34, Neither was there any among them that lacked: for as many as were possessors of lands or houses sold them, and brought the prices of the things that were sold,

Verse 35, And laid them down at the apostles feet: and distribution was made unto every man according as he had need.

Verse 36, and Jo-ses, who by the apostles was surnamed Barnabas, (which is, being interpreted, the son of consolation,) a Levite and of the country of Cyprus,

Verse 37, Having land, sold it, and brought the money, and laid it at the apostles feet.

As we can very well see in the book of acts, which is the beginning of the primitive church, with its original Christians this was the financial setup that they had established, of selling everything they had including lands, houses, all sorts of possessions, and putting the monies at the feet of the apostles.

And on verse 34, neither was there anyone among them that lacked, for as many as were possessors of lands or houses sold them, and brought the prices of the things that were sold, and laid them down at the apostles feet, and distribution was made unto every man according as he had need.

And distribution was made unto every man according as he had need, the wealth that they were receiving from the sale of these lands, these homes, and their possessions, it was daily distributed to the people according as they had need, that's why it says that there was nobody that had any kind of need because of this daily distribution, and this is what their financial procedures were.

Now if we go to acts chapter 2:41, 47 then they that gladly received his word were baptized: and the same day there were added unto them about 3000 souls.

Verse 42, And they continued steadfastly in the apostles doctrine and fellowship, and in the breaking of bread, and in prayers.

Verse 43, And fear came upon every soul: and many wonders and signs were done by the apostles.

Verse 44, And all that believed were together, and had all things common;

Verse 45, And sold their possessions and goods, and parted them to all men, as every man had need.

Verse 46, And they, continuing daily with one accord in the temple, and breaking bread from house to house, did eat their meat with gladness and singleness of heart,

Verse 47, Praising God, and having favor with all the people. And the Lord added to the church daily such as should be saved.

Now this was the original financial establishment for the local church, and even in churches that were being held from house to house. Now let's look at words like gladly, steadfastly, fellowship, breaking of bread, prayers, and had all things common, sold their possessions and goods, and parted them to all men, as every man had need, continuing daily with one accord, breaking bread from house to house, did eat their meat with gladness, singleness of heart, praising God, and having favor with all people, and the Lord added to the church daily as should be saved, noticed the prerequisite for church growth.

Now these words are definitely the prerequisite for an outpouring of the Holy Spirit upon the local church. It was the church's responsibility to take all this money whether it be a Tithe or an offering and supply every one of the member's needs,, the offering, the lands, the possessions that they sold was not so that the pastor would be very rich, and have a $10 million dollar home, and fly on a 30 or 40 million dollar plane, while half of the congregation has lost their job, and can even find food to eat, something is desperately wrong with the stewardship of these monies being brought into the local church.

It is very important to understand that I am not against the servant of God, the local ministers of God, a fivefold ministry gifts of God to be on barely get by Street, totally the opposite, I am pro-prosperity and financial stability for life.

My goal is to give you a balanced teaching in regards to Old Testament 10% tithes, versus New Testament, or under the new dispensation of grace giving all to the local church as it was in the early church. Now I'm not going to go into it but if you go to acts chapter 5:1, 11 where we see Ananias and Sapphira which sold their possession and kept back part of the price, and only brought in a certain part, and laid it at the apostles feet, but Peter said to Ananias why has Satan filled thine heart to lie to the Holy Ghost and to keep back part of the price of the land?

We know the whole story how Ananias and Sapphira died at the apostles feet, buy only bringing in a part of the price of the sale, instead of bringing the entire amount, they paid a hefty price, because all of the money had to be surrendered to the apostles, and there was no question about it, or either they would surrender all the money of the sale of their possession, or they would be severely judged and die in the process.

When we go to second Corinthians chapter 9:6, 11 But this I say, he which soweth sparingly shall reap also sparingly; and he which soweth bountifully shall reap also bountifully.

Verse seven, Every man according as he has purposed in his heart, so let him give; not grudgingly, or of necessity: for God loveth a cheerful giver.

Verse eight, And God is able to make all grace abound toward you; that ye, always having all sufficiency in all things, may abound to every good work:

Verse nine, (As it is written, he has dispersed abroad; he hath given to the poor: his righteousness remaineth forever.

Verse 10, Now he thatministereth seed to the sower both minister bread for your food, and multiply your seed sown, and increase the fruits of your righteousness;)

Verse 11, Being enriched in everything to all bountifulness, which causeth through us Thanksgiving to God.

The words that are important in these verses are sewing, in order to reap, and the word bountifully in order for us to reap bountifully, and the law of sowing and reaping.

Which is the only economy in God's kingdom that truly works, then it must be displayed with a cheerful heart knowing that you are sewing in God's kingdom and you will reap a harvest in do season if you faint not, and on verse eight it says that we always having sufficiency in all things, we may abound to every good work, and that is the end thereof, and then he goes on to say that we have dispersed abroad, and that we have given to the poor, and that our righteousness will remain forever. (Have we?)

A notice what it says on verse 10, God who ministers seed to the sower, will also minister bread for our food, and that God himself would multiply the seed sown, and the last thing he will do, he will increase the fruits of our righteousness. And this is tremendously good news.

Note God has always wanted us to have all sufficiency in order to meet all our needs, and help people around the world, and that is to be able to sow in the local church, or to sow in some body's ministry, or sow in someone's television program, or to sow in someone's rehabilitation program, or to sow in any missionary work around the world, the ultimate objective is that God will give it to you, if he can get it through you, God is trying to teach us, God is trying to make us, God is trying to use us, as a vessels of blessing to the local body of Christ, and in the interim showing us a beautiful law of sowing and reaping, for if we do that sow, we will not reap.

Now because we live in a modern society, and we need approximately $1,500-to $5,000 dollars a month to live, we are obviously not able to sow into God's Kingdom everything we own, houses, lands, and personal possessions, for we are not going to live under a bridge, so the least amount of money we should sow in God's kingdom is 10%, and the maximum, well we already talked about it, giving them everything, you be the judge, you be the cheerful giver, you be the sower, but the ultimate goal is to prove God to see if he will not open up the floodgates of heaven and pour us out a blessing we will not be able to contain.

The word redeemed means that God through the blood of Jesus Christ has repurchase us back to him, and we do not belong to ourselves, we have surrendered our wills to his, we have been translated from the demonic domain, and translated us into the kingdom of his dear son, Colossians chapter 1:13, 14, and we are God's family, and we are members of Christ's body, and we must understand, that includes our wallet also, and everything we Have been given and put in our hands, it includes our children, yes we do not own our children, they are placed in our care, so that we can instruct them, so that we can teach them, so that we can uphold them, so that we can teach the word of God to them, so that when they grow up they will not depart from the faith, and have a solid foundation for their convictions, we are only the stewards of it all. And the owners of nothing.

Yes we should learn God's economy, the law of sowing and reaping.

God wants us prosperous, God wants us believing him, God wants us sowing into his kingdom which is the local church, so that we may reap a good harvest, always having sufficiency in all things that we may abound to every good work.

THE # 18 THING I SHOULD DO IN CHRIST, (DISCOVER TWO KINDS OF FAITH)

The first one, is the passive one, is found in James chapter 1:5,8 If any of you lack wisdom, let him ask of God, that giveth to all men liberally, and upbraideth not; and it shall be given him.

Verse six, But let him ask in faith, nothing wavering, for he that waiver is like a wave of the sea driven with the wind and tossed.

Verse seven, For let not that man think that he shall receive anything of the Lord.

Verse eight, A double minded man is unstable in all his ways.

Here it says if any one of us lacks wisdom let him ask of God who gives liberally, and upbraided not, And it shall be given us, but let him ask in faith, nothing wavering, for the wavering person is like the wave of the sea driven with the wind and tossed.

Verse seven says, for let not that man think that he shall receive anything of the Lord, and on verse eight, says that a double minded man is unstable in all his ways.

How do we know that we are that person who will not receive anything of the Lord?
Now how do we know that we are that person that is wavering?

Now how do we know that we are that person who is a double minded?

The second one, is the active one, is found in James chapter 2:14, 17 What does it profit, my brethren, though a man say he has faith, and hath not works? Can faith save him?

Verse 15, If a brother or sister be naked, and destitute of daily food,

Verse 16, And one of you say on to them, depart in peace, be ye warmed and filled; notwithstanding ye give them not those things which are needful to the body; what doth it profit?

Verse 17, Even so faith, if it hath not works, is dead, being alone.

On the passive faith, you say you lack wisdom, but you don't read the Proverbs, which are full of God's wisdom, it is the wisdom of God in print, and we have no excuse not to read the Proverbs in order to obtain God's wisdom, but there is an action that requires us to do something from just sitting around watching television, there's a movement, a get up and do something, which is my responsibility in order to say that I have faith in God.

On the passive faith, you say that you are overweight, and that you need to lose weight, and that you need to stop eating excessive food, and to stay away from sweets.

But you don't even fast two times a week or even pray that God himself may strengthen your spirit, or go walking around the block so that you may sweat and loose that excessive overweight, or try to develop a different diet, different intake of food, your spirit has to govern your life, instead of your body ruling over you will, and leading you to slavery, people are bound. Faith without action is dead.

On the passive faith, people make all kinds over solution in the month of January after New Year's Day, and they only last 2 to 3 months and then they give up. Faith without works is dead.

In Hebrews chapter 11:1 Now faith is the substance of things hoped for, the evidence of things not seen, And on verse six, But without faith it is impossible to please him: for he that cometh to God must believe that he is, and that he is a rewarder of them that diligently seek him.

Now faith is, if we believe God, and we say that we have faith in God, and Jesus Christ is our Lord and Savior, then you and I have a measure of faith within us, Romans 12:3, the only way that measure of faith that was deposited within us will ever grow, it has to be now, that's why it starts now faith is. Now is the time to read the Proverbs in God's word to learn wisdom. Now is the time to get up from your sofa and after reading this book, put on some shoes to go walking around the block if you want to lose weight. Now is the time to stop eating and get rid of some of those suites within your refrigerator, and start making a diet for healthy intake into your body, now, now, now.

The substance of things hoped for, faith is substance, it's not wishful thinking, it's not preconceived ideas, it's not emotionalism, it's not the feelings, is an attitude that what we have prayed for, and are expecting to receive, it's already ours in Jesus name.

And that it is the evidence of the things that we have not yet seen, an attitude of gratefulness, and an attitude of thankfulness, and an attitude of appreciativeness, an attitude that is already mine, confessing it daily, believing it in my heart daily, and making it a fact within my heart, a done deal. And never praying for it again, but thanking God for it until it materializes.

Until what I have prayed for, goes from my head knowledge into my spirit and it becomes a part of me, never to doubt it ever again, or speak doubt or unbelief in regards to that which I have prayed for, now if it requires for me to do something, acting upon it in a heartbeat without doubting it. For Faith without action, works is dead alone.

Now on the active side of faith, faith without action cannot save us, in Romans chapter 10:9 we have to confess with our mouth the Lord Jesus, and believe in our hearts that God raised him from the dead, thou shall be saved, says the Bible.

So in James chapter 2:15, 16 begins as an illustration of a person that says that has faith, and sees a brother or a sister who is naked or has no food to eat, then says to him go in peace, be ye warmed and filled, not understanding that he has absolutely nothing for his body, what does it profit? Who is helped by this kind of attitude?

Now on the active site of faith, we need to get up and find a brother in Christ or a sister in Christ, or a physical family member that has need of food, or clothing, and go and help them, we need to get up and do something with what we say that we believe.

Are we living in a passive faith, or an active faith? If we are not doing something for someone, or if we are not praying at least for someone, if we are not feeding somebody, or clothing somebody, or being a channel where God bestows his blessings and it flows through us to others, then we are living in a passive faith, and not an active faith.

THE # 19 THING I SHOULD DO IN CHRIST, (DISCOVER TWO KINDS OF WISDOM)

The first one, is the passive wisdom, and it's the one that we ask God through prayer believing in our hearts and not doubting like a double minded person found in James chapter 1:5 and on this one we already talked about it, so were not going to go over it again.

Now on the active one is found in James chapter 3:13, 18 Who among you is wise and understanding? Let him show by his good behavior his deeds in the gentleness of wisdom.

Verse 14, But if you have bitter jealousy and selfish ambition in your heart, do not be arrogant and so lie against the truth.

Verse 15, This wisdom is not that which comes down from above, but is earthly, natural, demonic.

Verse 16, For where jealousy and selfish ambition exist, there is disorder and every evil thing.

Verse 17, But the wisdom from above is first pure, then peaceable, gentle, reasonable, full of mercy and good fruits, unwavering, without hypocrisy.

Verse 18, And the seed whose fruit is righteousness is sown in peace by those who make peace.

On the active wisdom it is required of every born-again believer to show by his good behavior his deeds in the gentleness of wisdom, but the Christians that are constantly bitter, constantly jealous, constantly selfish, and have selfish ambitions in their heart God is saying to not be arrogant and so lie against the truth, that is why it starts with who among you is wise and understanding? Here James the brother of Jesus calls it earthly, natural, and demonic.

Now on verse 16, he says that where jealousy and selfish ambition exist, there is disorder and every evil thing, it's very self-explanatory and it doesn't require a rocket scientist but this kind of wisdom does not come from God.

A lot of people like to justify their behavior, based on the hurts that they have experienced, or based on the wrong that other people have done to them, in order to operate in this kind of wisdom, or they are just flat out arrogant, self-exalted, and unrepentant.

And if this describes you, just bow your head for a simple prayer, and say out loud, dear heavenly father I come to you in Jesus name, please forgive me for being jealous and having selfish ambition in my heart, I don't want to be an arrogant individual, I don't want to have a high-end Almighty self-exalted spirit, I don't want to be an unrepentant Christian, I do not want to operate in the spirit of disobedience,

I ask you right now heavenly father in the name of Jesus to cleanse me with his precious blood, deliver me and cleanse me from all my unrighteousness, take away a high and mighty spirit from me, show me humility and love towards human beings, I do not want to live in this disorder and every evil thing, I want to be led by your precious Holy Spirit, and allow the fruit of the Spirit to operate in my life in Jesus name, amen.

THE # 20 THING I SHOULD DO IN CHRIST, (DISCOVER 2 KINDS OF TEMPTATION)

The first kind of temptation which is passive, is found in James chapter 1:13, 16 Let no one say when he is tempted, "I am being tempted by God"; for God cannot be tempted by evil, and he himself does not tempt anyone.

Verse 14, But each one is tempted when he is carried away and enticed by his own lust.

Verse 15, Then when lust has conceived, it gives birth to sin; and when sin is accomplished, it brings forth death.

Verse 16, Do not be deceived, my beloved brethren.

In this kind of temptation no one can ever say that they are tempted by God himself, for God cannot be tempted by evil, and he himself does not tempt anyone, it's the lust of the eyes, it's the lust of the flesh, and it is the pride of life that temps us, this is why it's so vitally important in this Temptation that we should close the eye gate, that we should close the emotional gate, and that we should close the ear gate into our bodies, and it is through these gates that the enemy is constantly tempting us to fall.

The second kind of temptation which is active, is found in James chapter 4:1, 5 What is the source of quarrels and conflicts among you? Is not the source your pleasures that wage war in your members?

Verse two, You lust and do not have; so you commit murder. And you are envious and cannot obtain; So you fight and quarrel. You do not have because you do not ask.

Verse three, You ask and do not receive, because you ask with wrong motives, so that you may spend it on your pleasures.

Verse four, Your adulteresses, do you not know that friendship with the world is hostility toward God? Therefore whoever wishes to be a friend of the world makes himself an enemy of God.

Verse five, Or do you think that the Scripture speaks to no purpose: "He jealously desires the spirit which he has made to dwell in us"?

This particular second kind of temptation, which speaks very loud to what happens in all of our members at one time or another, and it has absolutely nothing to do with the devil, and as we will study in this particular area of temptation, where we will realize that the poor devil has been blamed for a lot of things that our members themselves are the source.

We must always be sensitive in analyzing why we are angry, or why we are irritable, or why we are frustrated, and realize that the source of these quarrels and conflicts come from within us, it's the source of our pleasure that wages war within our members, and on verse two, we lust after things and we do not have, so what is it, that we normally do in the natural, we commit murder, and it is not necessarily a physical murder, but the murdering of our brothers and sisters character, and then we become very envious and we cannot obtain the things we so desperately are desiring, then we start praying and asking God for things, and we do not receive, because we ask with wrong motives, so that we may spend it on our pleasures.

And hear in James verse four, he calls us all adulteresses, for having friendship with this world which is hostility towards God, and it is this hostility towards God that causes our members to wage war within us thereby making us enemies of God.

He jealously desires the spirit which he has made to dwell in us, thereby not sharing us with the world and its systems of operation, there is a progressive sanctification that we need to slowly be doing as we develop our relationship with God spiritually, for God is a spirit, and they that worship him must worship him in spirit and in truth, you cannot be entangling yourself with the world and expect to have a perfect relationship with God spiritually, it just doesn't happen or either you are consecrated for the kingdom of God, or you are mingling and entangling yourself with this world, through drinking beer and smoking and dancing, you should not Be doing both, or either you belong to the kingdom of darkness, or you belong to the kingdom of his dear son, According to the scriptures Colossians chapter 1:13, 14 we have already been translated from the kingdom of darkness into the kingdom of God's dear son, so it is definitely our responsibility to live in, operate in, and move according to the kingdom principles that are found in Scripture's, and abstain from that which corrupts our minds and our flesh, it is our choice in what kingdom were going to operate in.

The # 21 thing that I should do in Christ, (discover 2 kinds of trusts) the first kind of trust which is passive, is found in James chapter 1:9, 11 But let the brother of humble circumstances glory in his high position;

Verse 10, and let the rich man glory in his humiliation, because like flowering grass he will pass away.

Verse 11, For the sun rises with a scorching wind, and withers the grass; and its flower falls off, and the beauty of its appearance is destroyed; so too the rich man in the midst of his pursuits will fade away.

Verse 12, Blessed is a man who perseveres under trial; for once he has been approved, he will receive the crown of life, which the Lord has promised to those who love him.

Is very clear that we see a person of humble circumstances and a rich man, and the analogy of both of them, the person of humble circumstances is a person who has a job, is married, has children, who has a normal home and is living a normal American lifestyle, and this person has made Jesus Christ his Lord and Savior, so he has placed his complete trust and belief system on God Almighty through Jesus Christ, this is a person with a prayer life, this is a person who goes to church, and when things get tough this person gets on his knees and trusts, and believes the promises of Almighty God which is his belief system, and God delivers him out of them all, there is a high position for the person of humble estate, in whose priorities are in order, and that is what we should glory on.

While on the other hand the rich person, and the medium to upper class whose priority is their job, their finances, their luxury, their automobiles, there material possessions, who never have any time for their moms and dads, or never have any time for their children, or never have any time for their husbands or their wives, who is constantly using a cheap excuse that they're working 12, 13,14, and 15 hours a day which according to today's society is the humblest thing they can do, will have to give God an account because of their lack of honoring moms and dads, those are the ones that will have to glory in their humiliation, because like flowering grass they will pass away, and when the sun comes up with a scorching wind and withers the grass, and flowers fall off, and the beauty of its appearance is destroyed, so too the rich man in the midst of their pursuits will fade away.

It is important to understand that the Bible is not against rich man, or women, it's saying that their priorities should be to seek first the kingdom of God and his righteousness, and make God Their priority, make God the one they trust the most, make God the source of their wealth and give God all of the glory for it, for after all it is God who gives us the wisdom to get wealth, not our smarts, and not our strength, it is putting Christ on the throne of the rich person's heart, and making God their Lord, and not the power of the riches and what it can get them, for it is easier for a camel to enter in the eye of a needle, than for a rich man to enter in the kingdom of God. Who do you put your faith and trust in?

Blessed is the man who perseveres under trials, for once he has been approved, he will receive the crown of life, which the Lord has prepared for those who love him.

Now the second kind of trust which is active, is found in James chapter 4:13, 17 Come now, you who say, "Today or tomorrow, we shall go to such and such a city, spend a year there and engage in business and make a profit."

Verse 14, yet you do not know what your life will be like tomorrow. You are just a vapor that appears for a little while and then vanishes away.

Verse 15, Instead, you ought to say, "If the Lord wills, we shall live and also do this or do."

Verse 16, But as it is, you boast in your arrogance; all such boasting is evil.

Verse 17, Therefore, to one who knows the right thing to do, and does not do it, to him it is sin.

Here we see the same decision-making out of priority, and leaving God out of the scene, and without acknowledging God making decisions to go here and there to do business make money and be rich, without the consent, without praying, without trusting, without making God their priority, not knowing that all we have for our lives is this moment, 10 minutes, two hours, 24 hours, five days, two weeks, one month, one year, three years in the future is not guaranteed to us, all we can believe for us, is in the here and now, and should ask God to preserve us, to give his visions and dreams, and if he wills to let us live a ripe old age according to Scriptures.

But either way we must always humble ourselves daily, and daily pray to God in the name of Jesus for everything we want, or everything we should do, and bring to God through prayer all the visions and dreams that are in our hearts already, in other words we need to get our heavenly father involved in our everyday affairs, and give him all the glory for the excellency and the victories that through Jesus Christ he has help us achieve, hallelujah.

Everybody that has their I in the throne room of their hearts, I am smart, I am intelligent, I am strong, I got this wealth, I did this study, I deserve this glory, I deserve this glamour, I deserve this appreciation of what my strength, and my knowledge, of my powers, have gotten me, and God says but as it is, you boost in your arrogance, you boast in yourself exalted spirit, and all such boasting is evil.

Instead of saying in Christ Jesus I am, in Christ Jesus I have, in Christ Jesus I can, in Christ Jesus I should, and thanks be to Jesus Christ who is my Lord and Savior, and through his strength, through his Revelation AL knowledge, and through this power, I have reached the top and have received all this success because of him, giving him all the glory.

Therefore, to the one who knows the right thing to do, and does not do it, to him it is sin.

THE # 22 THING I SHOULD DO IN CHRIST, (DISCOVER 2 KINDS OF ME)

The first kind of me is passive, and it's found in James chapter 1:8 But let the brother of humble circumstances glory in his high position.

The Brother or sister of humble circumstances has yielded his will to Christ's, and Jesus Christ is living on the throne room of his heart, thereby they should glory in the high position given to them by God in Christ, and this is what this book is about.

The second kind of me is active, and is found in James chapter 4:6, 10 but he gives a greater grace. Therefore it says, "God is opposed to the proud, but he gives grace to the humble."

Verse seven, Submit therefore to God. Resist the devil and he will flee from you.

Verse eight, Draw near to God and he will draw near to you. Cleanse your hands, you sinners; and purify your hearts, you double minded.

Verse nine, Be miserable and mourn and weep; let your laughter be turned into mourning, and your joy to gloom.

Verse 10, Humble yourselves in the presence of the Lord, and he will exalt you.

You don't have to be a rocket scientist to understand these verses, God opposes the proud, and gives grace to the person who humbles themselves enough to read up on his word and apply it to their lives, and be what God says that they are, what God says that they have, what God says that they can, and what God says that they should do in Christ.

When God says that we should resist the devil and he will flee from us, he is talking about our desires, our self-centered lifestyles, are egotistical proud full Outlook on ourselves, our unbiblical concept of ourselves, and when God says to draw near to him, to cleanse our hands, to purify our hearts, and he calls us a double minded person, is because on the throne room of our hearts we're divided as to who is the Lord of our lives, that is why he says to be miserable and mourn and weep, and to let our laughter be turned into mourning, and our joy into gloom, because the double minded person is unstable in all his ways and receives absolutely nothing from the Lord, and is no different than a slave, or a person in bondage.

There are two kinds of faith, the passive and the active. There are two kinds of wisdom, the passive and the active. There are two kinds of temptation, the passive and the active. There are two kinds of trusts, the passive and the active. There are two kinds of me on the throne room of my heart, the passive and active.

I think by now we should say a word of prayer, let us pray right now close your eyes, and say with me, dear heavenly father I come to you in the name of Jesus Christ of Nazareth, heavenly father I do not want to operate in a life of passive faith, I want to operate in the active life of faith, well up within my spirit, strength and my spirit, help me to operate in an active faith lifestyle, and put in practice everything I have read in this book, and get up and do what I can do in Christ, what I should do in Christ, for my spirit soul and body, and the well-being of every one of my family members in Jesus name. Amen

Dear heavenly father I come to you in Jesus name, and I am asking you to give me your wisdom, your revelation on knowledge, to practice what I have read in this book, and to read the book of Proverbs, to know your wisdom and act upon it.

In order to please you as your son, to be the best man of God in this planet, to be the best husband in this world, and to be the best father, to be the best provider for my family, and have the wisdom from heaven in order to get wealth and have good success, for it is your promise which you said in the book of Proverbs that the wages of the sinners are held up for the righteous, and finally heavenly father that I may be the best citizen of the United States of America and uphold the laws, pay my taxes on time, thereby becoming an outstanding role model for my family in Jesus Christ's name, Amen.

Now precious heavenly father please keep me from the temptation of my own lust, that I may not be seduced and enticed by it, and allow the source of my pleasures that war against my members take control of every part of my life and bringing me into bondage, strengthen the hidden man of my heart, give me a double portion of your anointing, visit my life right now empowering it with the precious Holy Spirit from the crown of my head to the soles of my feet, and precious heavenly father, in the name of Jesus come inside my house, fill every room of this house, and fill my entire being with your precious Holy Spirit, and that your Holy Spirit would deliver my mind from every ungodly influence, or from any tormenting demons, that your Holy Spirit will lead, will guide, will enlighten me, and let your Holy Spirit revealed to me when I'm going to make a mistake in Jesus name, amen.

Precious heavenly father I come to you in Jesus name, I do not want to put my trust in uncertain riches, but I want to put my full and absolute attention to you being the source of my supplies, whether it be in my spiritual life, my mental life, my physical life, my financial life, I want to put my full trust in you completely as my only source for everything.

And lastly heavenly father I want Jesus Christ of Nazareth to be the absolute lord of my heart, that I may remove the selfish, egotistical, self-centered, self-exalted I from the throne room of my heart, and that I may put the I am in Christ, I have in Christ, I can in Christ, and that I should do in Christ, giving him all the glory, giving him all the honor, giving him all the praise, for making me what I am today in Jesus name, amen.

Hallelujah, hallelujah, if you can lift both of your arms to the sky in an attitude of surrender Ness, and welcomed the precious Holy Spirit in your home, in your heart, in your life, in your marriage, and your family, welcomed the precious Holy Spirit and praise and glory him, I worship him inside this building where I'm recording this particular book. Precious heavenly father I give you honor, I give you glory, I give you adoration, you are worthy to be praised, you are worthy to be exalted, you are worthy to be magnified, you are worthy to receive honor wisdom and power, for yours is the kingdom and the power and the glory for ever and ever, amen.

NOW THE LAST THING I SHOULD DO IN CHRIST, (SELF-EVALUATE)

If our religion does not reveal the leader, this is found in second Corinthians chapter 5:19 something is wrong.

If our religion does not manifest its leader, this is found in the gospel of John chapter 1:14 something is wrong.

If our religion does not personalize the leader, this is found in the gospel of John chapter 1:12 something is wrong.

If our religion doesn't give me communication with the leader, this is found in the gospel of John chapter 14:13, 14 something is wrong.

If our religion doesn't forgive its members sins, this is found in the gospel of John chapter 3:16 something is wrong.

If our religion does not liberate its members from doubt, unbelief, rejection, unworthiness, low self-value, low self-worth, low self-esteem, this is found in the gospel of Luke chapter 4:18, 19 something is wrong.

If our religion does not seal its members inside the heart, and this is found in Ephesians chapter 1:13, 14 something is wrong.

If our religion does not implant a divined nature, and this is found in second Peter chapter 1:2, 9 something is wrong.

If our religion does not translate us from the wrong kingdom of darkness and into the kingdom of his dear son, and this is found in Colossians chapter 1:13, 14 something is wrong.

If our religion does not baptize us with the power, and this is found in acts chapter 1:8 something is wrong.

If our religion does not baptize us with the leader's nature which is love, and this is found in first to the Corinthians chapter 13:3, 6 something is wrong.

If our religion does not baptize us with the leaders fruits that are found in Galatians chapter 5:22, 23 and something is wrong.

If our religion does not baptize us with the gifts of the spirit found in first Corinthians chapter 12:7, 11 something is wrong.

If our religion does not give us all role to play in the body of his son found in first Corinthians chapter 12:18, 20 something is wrong.

If our religion does not give us a mission to fulfill around the world and this is found in Matthew chapter 28:19, 20 something is wrong.

If our religion does not give us a title for representation found in second Corinthians chapter 5:20 something is wrong.

If our religion does not give us a method for spiritual growth found in Romans chapter 12 1:3 something is wrong.

If our religion doesn't help us to be like the image of our leader found this first John chapter 4:17 something is wrong.

If our religion does not hear our prayers daily found in first Corinthians chapter 5 verse 14, 15 something is wrong.

If the leader of our religion does not protect us and pray for us daily found in the gospel of John chapter 17: 15 something is wrong.

If the leader of our religion does not give us a new seed within us to have victory over the world found in first John chapter 5: 1 something is wrong.

If the leader of our religion along with his father doesn't come to live within us found in the gospel of Matthew chapter 14:23 something is wrong.

If the leader of our religion does not give us a new heart, and a new spirit, within us found in Ezekiel chapter 36:28, 28 something wrong.

If the leader of our religion doesn't promise to never leave us nor for sakes us found in Hebrews 13:5 something id wrong.

If the leader of our religion does not make as a member of his church, which the gates of hell shall not prevail against it found in Matthew's chapter 16:18 something is wrong.

If the leader of our religion does not give us authority, and power against serpents and scorpions and over all the power of the enemy found in Luke chapter 10:19, 20 something is wrong.

If the leader of our religion does not give us triumph over the spiritual realm, and delegates that authority to us found in Colossians chapter 2:12, 15 something is wrong.

If the leader of our religion does not cause us to always triumph over every battle and circumstance in our lives, found in second Corinthians chapter 2:14 something is wrong.

If the leader of our religion does not give us an identity after our spiritual rebirth found in the gospel of John chapter 1:11, 13 something is wrong.

If the leader of our religion does not guarantee us that in battle nothing shall separate us from his love found in Romans chapter 8:35, 39 something is wrong.

If the leader of our religion doesn't guarantee us that in his name we are more than conquerors found in

If the leader of our religion does not reveal to us his supernatural wisdom and knowledge found in the book of Proverbs chapter 3:13, 18 something is wrong.

If the leader of our religion does not reveal to us the true knowledge of the past present and future of everything created found in the gospel of John chapter 1:1, 14 something is wrong.

If the leader of our religion does not reveal to us the origin of everything created found in Genesis chapter 1:1, 31 something is wrong.

If the leader of our religion does not guarantee that one day he will come back to take us home found in first Thessalonians chapter 4:13, 18 something is wrong.

If the leader of our religion does not take us home and give us a glorified body so that we can come and reign with him on the earth for a millennial reign found in the book of revelations chapter 20:6 something is wrong.

If the leader of our religion does not give us an inheritance through his love letter written and found in Hebrews chapter 9:12, 17 something is wrong.

If the leader of our religion does not give us everything we have been talking about absolutely free and without any merit or works found in Ephesians chapter 2:8, 9 something is wrong.

And lastly if the leader of our religion under the dispensation of grace does not let us live through unmerited favor found in Ephesians chapter 1:10, 14 something is wrong.

And thank God we don't have a religion, but we have a relationship with Jehovah God, through the shed blood of his son Jesus Christ on the cross, and the baptism in the Holy Spirit with the fruit of the spirit, and the gifts of the spirit to be victorious human beings on this planet, overcoming every attack and situations in our lives and being more than conquerors through him that loved us, in Jesus name amen.

All of these attributes are freely given to every human being that repents of their sin, accepts the death burial and resurrection of Jesus Christ on the cross, and invites Jesus Christ to come into this heart, and then be filled with the Holy Spirit of promise, then and only then can you receive all of these attributes that we just previously mentioned, only in the Christian faith can you have a daily relationship with your maker and Creator of all things.

Now if your religion forces you to love the leader, and hate peoples of all other religion, that is not from God.

Now if your religion forces you to submit against your will to destroy other person that is not from God.

Now if your religion forces you to read its book, to obtain methods for self-destruction that is not of God.

If your religion forces you to do anything, forces you to think a specific way, or forces you to act like anything abnormal, or else they will excommunicate you from the leader, that is not from God.

If your religion forces you to submit to an idol, made like a human being, or an animal, that is not of God.

If your religion forces you to communicate in a particular manner with that idol, that is not from God.

If your religion forces you to pledge allegiance, and offer sacrifices, to that particular idol, that is not of God.

If your religion forces you to hate, Reject, mistreat, forsake, abandon any family members because they don't practice that believe system that is not of God.

If your religion forces you to kill humans in order to receive something from its leader, or from heaven, that is not of God.

If your religion forces you to hate your government enough to be a terrorist against it, that is not from God.

If your religion doesn't teach you to pray for your enemies, that is not from God.

If your religion causes you to be self-exalted, make you self-righteous, and makes you force other people to serve you, that is not from God.

If your religion causes you to break the law, it's not from God.

If your religion causes you to break your sense of reality, it is not from God.

If your religion causes you do drugs for hallucinations in order to perform, that is not from God.

If this describes your belief system this is not from God.

Dear God in heaven, father of Abraham Isaac and Jacob, I come to you in Jesus name your son, asking you to forgive me, I turn my back on idol worship, I turn my back on any other God other than Jehovah God, in Jesus name, I repent of my sins, and ask you to deliver my mind from wrong religions, that have influenced me, and caused me to go astray, I invite Jesus Christ into my heart to save me right now, please Lord baptize me with the Holy Spirit of promise, and give me your fruits and gifts, in Jesus name.

If you prayed that prayer, I believe you got born again, and so welcome to God's family

All you have to do now is just join a full gospel church, confess to everyone that you are a Christian, and may God richly bless you.

I hope that this first edition of (who am I), in Christ Jesus has turned your life completely around for after all that has been my greatest, and most important goal in this book, in Jesus, name amen.

www.ingramcontent.com/pod-product-compliance
Lightning Source LLC
LaVergne TN
LVHW041908070526
838199LV00051BA/2546